Life On Your Terms

By

Ken Mahoney

ISBN 978-0-9980047-1-6

This publication contains the opinions and ideas of the author. It is sold with the understanding that neither the author nor publisher is engaged in rendering legal, tax, investment, insurance, financial, accounting, or other professional advice or services. If a reader requires such advice or services, a competent professional should be consulted. References to organizations have been given for the purpose of information and do not constitute a recommendation. Any perceived slights of specific people or organizations are unintentional.

No warranty is made with respect to the accuracy or completeness of the information contained herein, and both the author and publisher specifically disclaim any responsibility for any liability, loss or risk, personal or otherwise, which is incurred as a consequence, directly or indirectly, by the use of any of the contents of this book. While the information and advice in this book are believed to be accurate and true at the time of publication, neither the author, publisher or distributor can guarantee results nor accept any responsibility or liability for any damage or losses of any kind resulting from any advice included in this guide, be it from the author, any person or persons mentioned in this book, or any product, listing or mention, whether directly or indirectly.

The mission of Mahoney Asset Management
Know our clients well
Anticipate their needs
Exceed their expectations!

Contents

About The Author – Ken Mahoney

Investor, author of 7 books including *A GPS for Your Retirement*,

 and licensed financial advisor for more than 27 years, Ken Mahoney is the CEO of Mahoney Asset Management where he offers clients tailored retirement solutions. Using data provided by the leading financial research companies, Morningstar and Standard and Poor's, Mahoney Asset Management provides detailed performance analysis and investment recommendations for goals like preparing to leave your job, purchasing a second home, or planning for retirement.

Because of Ken's comprehensive financial expertise, he is sought after by CNBC, Fox Business News, ABC and The Today Show to speak on topics such as planning for retirement and stock market investment strategies. Ken has also been a staple on morning, drive time radio, providing financial advice for the past 24 years to listeners in the local New York City Market and can be found  on America's Weekend, a financial radio program that is syndicated to over 1500 radio stations throughout the country. Having been recruited to serve on the House of Representatives Banking and Financial Services Committee, he advised the Chairperson of the Committee, Congresswoman Sue Kelly, on the impact of new financial regulations, Federal Reserve Bank transparency, and guided the Committee in asking questions of Alan Greenspan.

A believer in giving back, Ken has been serving his community for more than two decades volunteering as a member of Meals On Wheels and The United Way. Ken is the former Chairman of the Board at Make-A-Wish Foundation, and currently serves as chairman of the alumni board. Acknowledged by the New York State Legislature for his dedication and outstanding community service, Ken was honored with a Distinguished Service Award and chosen by Rockland County as community leader of the year.
In addition to his work as a financial advisor and community leader, Ken is a successful Broadway producer and investor. Ken won the Tony Award of Best Revival of a Musical as producer of *Pippin and Gershwin's Porgy and Bess*, and was nominated for a Grammy Award for producer of the Best Musical Theater Album *Matilda* and *Nice Work*. Ken is also a three time Emmy Award winner for his work as producer on the television show *Due Process*.

Ken and his wife Trish have been married since he proposed to her in 1994 on the ice skating rink under Rockefeller Center Christmas tree. They have two sons, Brendan and Connor, for whom Ken coaches' baseball and soccer. When not working for his clients, Ken can be found writing and reading several books per week like *The Snowball Warren Buffet and the Business of Life*; *Shark Tales*; and *David and Goliath*: *Underdogs, Misfits*, and the *Art of Battling Giants*.

Introduction

"Can I afford to retire?"

Almost every day for the past 28 years in my financial planning practice, I have been asked that question by a client or a caller to my radio and TV program - and the answer usually is, "It depends." That's because there is no one "right" answer to that question, and there are many different variables that will also come into play when figuring it out.

It's likely that you've seen or read various retirement planning "rules" in the media. Some of these will tell you that you should have a certain dollar amount saved in order to retire. Others will tell you that you need at least 70% of your pre-retirement earnings coming in so that you can live comfortably after your employer's paycheck stops.

You may have also heard that you have to wait until you are 65, 70, or even older in order to be financially independent, retired, and living life the way you want to be living it and doing what you want to do.

But the truth is that every situation is different, and it really is dependent upon how much you will spend in retirement, where you decide to live, what income sources you will have available, the future rate of inflation, and when you opt to take that step into the next phase of your life.

You may also be in a situation where the timing of your retirement isn't up to you. For instance today, there are many companies that are still "downsizing," leaving those who are in their 50s and 60s suddenly without employment. Likewise, as a part of the "sandwich generation," you may be forced into leaving the workforce to care for an ailing parent or other loved one.

If this is you, then you may be wondering if you will realistically be able to retire now. That's why it is so important to have your own unique plan in place. In order to get our clients where they want to go, we've developed a GPS system. This program not only helps to determine where you currently are from a financial standpoint, but it also provides direction on how to get where you want to go.

Much like the GPS system that you may use in your travels, our system can also give you information on whether or not you are on track, and what detours you may need to take if anything along the journey has changed.

Dreaming vs. Planning

When you close your eyes and imagine your ideal retirement, what exactly do you see? Are you relaxing in a new beach house, playing endless rounds of golf on courses around the world, or sightseeing on numerous road trips while at the same time visiting with family and friends?

Everyone is different, which is why everyone's perfect retirement dream will be different, too. When I'm meeting with clients in person, as well as fielding questions on the radio or TV, I hear from people who have a wide variety of different retirement dreams.

Because all retirement goals can be different, though, there is no one-size-fits all solution to get you where you want to go financially in the future. However, one thing is for sure. That is, everyone needs to have a plan.

Becoming financially independent is a journey - and just like any other trip that you would take, you will need to map out a plan in order to ensure that you get where you want to go. The plan will also let you know whether or not you're on track to get to your ultimate destination, and if there are any roadblocks that you need to avoid along the way.

Everyone likes to dream about what their ideal retirement will look like. But for many, the dreaming phase is where it all stops. By putting a well-defined financial plan in place, though, your retirement dream can become that much more of a reality.

Anything is Possible

In August 2016, 34-year-old Brandon - who is also known as the Mad Fientist blogger - retired. He was able to walk away from his employer and start living life on his terms - and he was able to do so by setting up and following a clearly defined plan.

What makes Brandon's story even more interesting, though, is that for the first several years of his career, he wasn't even saving for anything in particular. "Retirement" seemed like a long way away - especially for someone who was in his 20s - and he knew that he should be putting some money away for that time "in the future" when he would need it.[1]

6

But, once Brandon learned more about achieving financial independence, he realized that you don't necessarily have to wait until you are in your 60s or 70s to retire. In fact, if your money is working hard enough and you have the proper plan in place, you can retire at any time. So he did!

By living frugally and saving well, he was able to reach his goal early in life. But he wouldn't have been able to do so without a good, solid plan that allowed him to track exactly where he was in terms of savings, investments, liabilities, and overall finances along the way.[2]

In Brandon's case, he set up a series of spreadsheets that provided him with the following information:

- Account Balances
- Investments
- Net Worth
- Monthly Expenses[3]

The most important spreadsheet, though, was one titled Financial Independence. This one broke down how many more years he would need to work in order to pay for specific expenses indefinitely.[4]

What made this information even more powerful is that it showed just how many years of his life he was essentially "trading" in order to have certain items, and because of that, he was able to decide whether or not the purchase or the ongoing monthly expense was really worth it.[5]

Financial Independence Spreadsheet

	A	B	C	D	E	F	G	H	I
1									
2		Starting Balance	$474,859						
3		Withdrawal Rate	3.85%						
4		Inflation-Adjusted Growth Rate	5.00%						
5									
6		Annual Income (post tax)	$60,754.92						
7		Annual Savings	$28,750.92						
8		Savings Rate	47.32%						
9									
10				Totals:	$87.68	$2,667.00	$32,004.00	$831,272.73	5.85
11									
12		Item	Cost		Daily	Monthly	Annually	Required Savings	Years till FI
13									
14		Mortgage	$582.00		$19.13	$582.00	$6,984.00	$181,402.60	1.28
15		Internet	$49.00		$1.61	$49.00	$588.00	$15,272.73	0.11
16		Cell Phone	$10.00		$0.33	$10.00	$120.00	$3,116.88	0.02
17		Propane	$402.00		$13.22	$402.00	$4,824.00	$125,298.70	0.88
18		Electricity	$70.00		$2.30	$70.00	$840.00	$21,818.18	0.15
19		Groceries	$336.50		$11.06	$336.50	$4,038.00	$104,883.12	0.74
20		Car Insurance	$0.00		$0.00	$0.00	$0.00	$0.00	0.00
21		Home Insurance	$0.00		$0.00	$0.00	$0.00	$0.00	0.00
22		Property Tax	$273.00		$8.98	$273.00	$3,276.00	$85,090.91	0.60
23		Gasoline	$254.50		$8.37	$254.50	$3,054.00	$79,324.68	0.56
24		Car	$0.00		$0.00	$0.00	$0.00	$0.00	0.00
25		House	$0.00		$0.00	$0.00	$0.00	$0.00	0.00
26		Misc.	$75.00		$2.47	$75.00	$900.00	$23,376.62	0.16
27		Health Insurance	$157.00		$5.16	$157.00	$1,884.00	$48,935.06	0.34
28									
29		Restaurants	$332.50		$10.93	$332.50	$3,990.00	$103,636.36	0.73
30		Entertainment	$34.00		$1.12	$34.00	$408.00	$10,597.40	0.07
31		Shopping	$0.00		$0.00	$0.00	$0.00	$0.00	0.00
32		Travel	$75.00		$2.47	$75.00	$900.00	$23,376.62	0.16
33		Gifts	$16.50		$0.54	$16.50	$198.00	$5,142.86	0.04
34									
35									

Source: Business Insider

Brandon and his wife are now planning to travel and see the world - and they didn't have to wait for another 30 years in order to achieve their dream. But, none of it would be possible without a plan.

Facing Up To Your Finances

What we have seen and learned from working with hundreds of people throughout almost three decades is that in order to get where you want to go financially, you need to have a starting point. This is the first step to arriving at your future destination.

In some cases, however, people don't know where they are. They know that they should be saving for "the future," but there is really no set method or plan for doing so. While this may be a good start, not knowing where you are starting from won't help get you to your goal, because you won't have a sense of how far away that goal actually is.

In other instances, people may be afraid of what their financial future holds. This could be due to a lack of savings, previous losses in the market, substantial amounts of debt, or even simply because they are unsure of which way to turn.

But the worst thing that you can do is ignore your financial issues, because they won't just "go away." Instead, facing your finances head on with a well-defined plan and clear cut goals is the way to get on track.

Will Retiring Now Be Possible for You?

Successfully arriving at any destination requires a good sense of where you're starting from. It will also be necessary to be emotionally prepared for your new life, new routine, and sense of purpose.

Then from there, you can build and chart your course. While retiring right away may not be possible for everyone, we can all take some lessons from Brandon the Mad Fientist's experience, knowing that a good map can lead you to where you want to be.

Regardless of how much you have been able to save in the past, where you are right now is simply a starting point. That's why having the retirement GPS system is so essential. It will provide you with your own personalized projection.

It will also help you in ensuring that you'll have what you need in order to keep pace with future inflation and potential health care costs, as well as other possible challenges that may come along.

In order to get an accurate route, though, you need to know where you are starting from right now and where you want to end up. Our unique GPS system will provide you with the answers that you need. Once you have your route programmed in, you will be on your way to turning your retirement dreams into a reality.

So, let's get stated.

*Note: *While the concepts in this book are helpful, they are general in nature. For a more personalized plan, contact us. We run several promotions each year, where these GPS projections are free of charge.*

Sources

1. "A man who retired at 34 shares a spreadsheet that helped him get there. Business Insider. Aug. 19, 2016.
(http://www.businessinsider.com/mad-fientist-early-retirement-spreadsheet-2016-8/#tab-1-balances-1)

2. Ibid.

3. Ibid.

4. Ibid.

5. Ibid.

Chapter 1: Know Where You Are Now

If you've ever been driving in unknown territory, then you are likely familiar with turning on your GPS device, plugging in the address of your destination, and then following the directions to get where it is that you want to go.

But in order to provide you with the best route, it is essential that you also enter in where you currently are, because if you don't, then you could end up going way off course. In fact, even with the best GPS device, not having a proper starting point won't allow it to offer the solution you need.

It's also important to have the most updated GPS application. That's because there may be new roads to take, or alternatively, roads that are either under construction – or no longer available to you at all. Planning for retirement can be a similar process.

The Changing Nature of Retirement

When it comes to planning your best route to retirement, you will need to have a good idea of what you want to do when you get there. While many people dream about how it will be when they can control their time, having a successful retirement will require that you have a purpose, and that you are emotionally prepared.

If you've worked for most of your life, you may see yourself as being "what you do." In other words, many people - whether intentionally or unintentionally - define themselves by their career.

But, starting on the day that you retire, that will all change. So, it is essential to still have goals, activities, and an overall sense of purpose even after you leave your employer. Doing so can make each and every day in retirement more rewarding.

You will also need to know what is and isn't an option for you. What used to provide the retirees of yesterday with the income that was needed may not be open to you today. In fact, the way in which we retire has changed considerably over time. In the past, retirees typically had three key income sources. These included a defined benefit pension, Social Security, and personal savings and investments.

Disappearing Pension Income

Up until just a couple of decades ago, many companies offered defined benefit pensions to their employees. In a defined benefit pension plan, as the name implies, the amount of the benefit that is paid out to the recipient is known. Therefore, a retiree could count on a certain amount of guaranteed income from this type of plan, often for the remainder of their life.

An added perk to participating in a defined benefit pension plan is that the responsibility for investment gains and losses is up to the employer – not the employee – as is ensuring that there is enough income for the retiree.

This is unlike the defined contribution plans that are more apt to be offered by employers today. In a defined contribution plan, the amount of money that an employee may contribute into the plan is capped. In addition, the amount of retirement income that is generated from the plan is also up to the employee.

Unfortunately, due in large part to the massive expense of keeping defined benefit pension plans in place, many companies have done away with these benefits and replaced them with defined contribution plans. The most popular of these is the 401(k).

Uncertain Social Security

Another key source of retirement income for many retirees will come from Social Security. If you have enough work credits (40 "quarters," or ten years), and you have paid taxes into the system, then you will qualify for retirement benefits from this source.

But, while Social Security can be a way for you to receive lifetime retirement income, it was never intended to be a retiree's only source. And, in most cases, the amount will not be enough to provide you with the lifestyle you hope for in retirement.

According to the Social Security Administration, "Social Security was never meant to be the only source of income for people when they retire. Social Security replaces about 40 percent of an average wage earner's income after retiring."[1] In addition to Social Security only replacing a portion of your pre-retirement wages, there has been a great deal of speculation as to just how long this program can remain financially solvent.

Personal Savings and Investments

The other component of retirement income will often include personal savings and investments. While many retirees in the past did not need to rely solely on this particular source of income generation, today it is becoming much more important. This is especially the case given the disappearance of defined benefit pension plans, as well as the uncertainty that surrounds Social Security.

What You Own and What You Owe

In order to determine just exactly where you currently stand in terms of your finances, and to come up with your "starting point," it is important to come up with good, solid figure on how much you own and how much you owe. The best way to do this is to create a list of your assets and liabilities.

Assets

Assets are defined as being items that have economic value and that are expected to provide future benefit. There are a wide variety of items that can be considered as assets – and, after adding up the value of all that you own, you may be surprised at their overall worth.

Some assets that you may own can include the following:

- Personal Savings
- Personal Investments
- Retirement Plan Assets
- IRA(s)
- Personal Residence
- Rental Property
- Vacation Home
- Collectibles (art, coins, stamps, etc.)
- Jewelry
- Automobile

Liabilities

While assets are things that you own, liabilities are what you owe – or debt obligations. Some examples of your liabilities can include:

- Home mortgage
- Home equity loan
- Auto loan(s)
- Personal loan(s)
- Credit card balance(s)

By adding up the total amount of your assets and subtracting the amount of your total liabilities, you will come up with your overall net worth.

Taking Advantage of Saving and Investment Opportunities

By taking advantage of saving and investment opportunities, you can increase the amount of your assets – and, provided that you keep the amount of your liabilities in check, you can also increase the amount of your total net worth.

One of the best ways that you can greatly increase the amount in your asset column is to participate in your employer's retirement plan (if this is an option for you). There can be a number of advantages to doing so.

If your employer offers a 401(k) plan, for example, you may defer your contributions. This means that you can reduce the amount of taxable income that you have for each year by the amount that you've contributed to your retirement plan.

In 2016, you can contribute up to $18,000 to your 401(k) plan, if you are age 49 or younger. If, however, you are age 50 or older, you can contribute an additional $6,000 in "catch up" contribution.

Many 401(k) plans will provide a variety of different investment options for you to choose from. These may include:

- Money Market Funds
- Stock and bond mutual funds
- Your own company's stock

These can all offer varying degrees of risk and reward potential, so employees can choose which option or options will work the best for them, depending on specific goals.

In addition, the growth on your 401(k) funds will be tax-deferred. This means that there are no taxes due on the gain within the account. In fact, you won't be taxed on this money until the time your withdraw it.

Another nice benefit that is associated with 401(k) retirement plans is the fact that many employers will "match" a percentage of their employees' contributions. This is often referred to as "free money." If your employer offers a matching contribution, you could obtain additional funds in your account over and above your personal deferrals.

Assessing Your Retirement Ability

In planning for retirement and determining where you are now, it is essential to get a "snap shot" of your finances. However, there are other factors that are also important in helping you to prepare for this time in your life. This is because other criteria will have an impact on how much retirement income you may require.

Health Factors

Your health can be an extremely important factor as it relates to your finances in retirement. This is because it can affect what you are able to do, as well as how much you will be spending from your income sources.

For example, a recent survey conducted by Fidelity estimated that a 65-year-old couple retiring in 2016 will need an estimated

$260,000 to cover health care costs in retirement. This is a 6% increase over the prior year's estimate of $245, 000. (2)

While Medicare will help to cover some of these costs, those who are enrolled in Medicare will still have a number of out-of-pocket copayments and deductibles that they are responsible for paying.

As an example, Medicare Part A covers hospitalization expenses. However, (in 2016) Medicare Part A also has a deductible of $1,288 for each benefit period. In addition, for those who incur lengthy hospital stays, there is also a $322 coinsurance cost per day for days 61 through 90. And, if you have used up all of your "lifetime reserve days" on your Medicare coverage, you could also incur a coinsurance amount of $644 per day beyond the 91st day.

The $260,000 in health care costs do not take into account the possibility of needing long-term care – although it is estimated that 7 in 10 retirees who are over age 65 will need at least some form of long-term care services in their lifetime.(3)

This care can also be extremely expensive. According to Genworth's 2016 Cost of Care Survey, the national median daily rate for a private room in a skilled nursing facility is $253. (4) This equates to over $92,000 per year.

Even the need for home health care for basic assistance with everyday activities such as bathing and dressing can be quite costly. On average, the national median hourly rate for home health aide and homemaker services is $20 per hour in 2016.(5) Unfortunately, Medicare pays very little for skilled nursing facility care, and even less for home health care services.

For instance, even if you qualify for Medicare's skilled nursing home benefit, you could still be responsible for paying a substantial amount in terms of coinsurance. That is because during the first 20 days of your stay, provided that you qualify, Medicare will pay the tab.

However, after day 20, the following coinsurance charges would apply (in 2016):

- Days 21 through 100: $161 per day
- Day 101 and beyond: The patient is responsible for all costs.(6)

Because of the potential need for health care in retirement, combined with the vast expense, these costs will also need to be anticipated and prepared for as you create your financial roadmap for the future.

Desire, Need and Ability to Work

Even though many people may consider retirement as a time to stop working, having a paid position may be something that you will need or want to do down the road. For some, starting a new business or taking on a job in a different field is something that is anticipated.

For others, however, due to the need for additional income to cover living expenses, working in retirement may actually be a necessity. With that in mind, it will be important to get an approximate calculation of how much you will need for your living expenses in retirement, and then determine how much you will have coming in from various sources. If you find that there is a "gap," now is the time to make a plan for filling in the additional income you will require.

Are You Prepared to Move Forward?

Given the amount of expense that you could incur, are you prepared to do what is needed in order to achieve retirement security? Moving forward can require setting clear cut goals - both financially and emotionally - and then doing what it takes in order to accomplish them.

But, while you may be excited about getting to your goals, for some people, there can be a disconnect between the expectations that you maintain for your retirement and the financial actions that you have actually taken in order to get there.

There may also be gap between what you think you will need financially in order to retire as versus what you actually have. Because of this, you may not feel confident that you will be able to afford retirement.

Getting to your milestone can therefore require you to get into the proper mindset as you move forward. In doing so, you will then be better prepared to take the financial actions that you need in order to achieve your goals.

Having the right mindset, coupled with a good solid plan, can get you going in the right direction. It will also help to keep you on the right track when things get difficult or you feel you are going off course.

Sources

1. Social Security Administration
   (https://www.ssa.gov/pubs/EN-05-10024.pdf)
2. "Health Care Costs for Couples in Retirement Rise to an
   Estimated $260,000, Fidelity Analysis Shows." Aug. 16,
   2016. (https://www.fidelity.com/about-fidelity/employer-
   services/health-care-costs-for-couples-in-retirement-rise)
3. Ibid.
4. Genworth Cost of Care Survey 2016.
   (https://www.genworth.com/dam/Americas/US/PDFs/Con
   sumer/corporate/131168_050516.pdf)
5. Ibid.
6. Medicare.gov (https://www.medicare.gov/your-medicare-
   costs/costs-at-a-glance/costs-at-glance.html#collapse-
   4808)

Chapter 2: Know Where You Want to Go

One of the primary factors in determining whether or not you can afford to retire is knowing what type of lifestyle you want to live in the future. This will include determining your sense of purpose and what you want to do in order to fulfill it.

Being able to retire will also encompass deciding where you want to live, what type of activities you want to participate in, and approximately how long you may need your retirement income to last.

While many financial advisors may tell you that you should ideally bring in 70% of your pre-retirement wages in order live comfortably, this is not necessarily the case for everyone. Because everybody's idea of the ideal retirement differs, our experience has shown that for some people it will take less than 70%, and in others it may take more.

Likewise, just simply saving and investing without any real purpose will not typically get you where you want to go either. Imagine if you just got in your car and started driving around, with no clear purpose.

This is why it is so important to know where you want to go - and the GPS system can help you to establish your projected route. In doing so, you can then plan for what you need, based on where you are starting from right now. You will also be able to determine if or when you will need to make adjustments along the way.

Determining What is Important to You

For many people, when it comes to planning for the future, it is assumed that there are just two distinct phases in life. These are your working years and your retirement years. In the past, our working years encompassed the larger of these two phases.

But today, due in large part to longer life expectancies, it is not unusual to see retirement lasting for 20, 30, or more years. And, depending on when you are actually able to take that step, the number of years that you spend in retirement may even be more than the number of years that you spent working.

Because of that, it is essential to have a good, solid plan in place. But, in addition to just simply looking at that plan in terms of dollars and cents, it will also be important to design and create that plan in conjunction with what is important to you.

While you may be excited to move on to the next phase of your life, leaving behind a successful career can be difficult. Once you exit the working world, you may feel that you no longer have that sense of belonging - whether it be to your company, your industry, or even your own self-worth.

For that reason, it will be essential to set some personal goals for what is meaningful to you. That may include volunteering for a favorite charity, starting a brand new business, or visiting all of the major league baseball stadiums across the U.S. Knowing your purpose going forward can help you in knowing how much income or resources you will require.

Although the account types and investments that are used by many financial professionals are often the same, the way in which they are used will usually differ, based on the goals that you are trying to achieve.

Some financial advisors will simply offer you products, based on projected return or because it seems like a "good deal." But just purchasing a variety of financial products with no connection to each other - or to your overall goals - is not the best path for getting to your ultimate destination.

Just like when you're following a map, you need to have a specific purpose for taking each road in the process of getting to your end goal. One road may lead you somewhere, but another will lead you somewhere else. And, if there's no correlation, you could find yourself just driving around in circles.

With that in mind, it is important to first determine what is important to you. Being able to retire will require that you have enough money to pay your bills. But having a truly successful retirement will also require you to have a purpose. Starting with your purpose, then, you will be able to more clearly define and set your goals.

Setting Your Goals

People ask me all the time what is the best thing that they can do in order to prepare for retirement. Although there are many things that can be done to prepare, I tell them that the very best thing is to develop a plan, and then to work that plan consistently. The clearer your vision is, the better you will be able to develop your plan and set specific retirement goals.

One of the best ways to start setting your goals is to ask yourself what your ideal day would look like when you retire. For example, where will you be living? What will you do when you wake up? Who will you be surrounded by? What type of place will you be living in?

All of these questions will help you in setting your retirement goals, and in turn, based on all of your answers, will also be important in determining how much savings or income you will need in order to accomplish them.

You can set both long- and short-term goals. In fact, based on your long-term goals, your GPS tracking system will provide you with a "map" - and many of the points along your route will require that short-term goals also be met.

For instance, if one of your ultimate retirement goals is to purchase a home by the beach, then shorter-term goals such as saving a certain amount of money each month or year will typically be required.

Although everyone's financial goals may differ, the difference between long- and short-term goals are that long-term goals will generally take you more than five years to accomplish. Some examples of long-term goals may include:

- Purchasing a vacation home
- Paying off all of your debts
- Living solely off the income from your investments

Short-term goals, on the other hand, are those that may only take a year or less to achieve. Some examples of these can be:

- Saving for the down payment on a new car
- Renovating your kitchen
- Funding your IRA

Once you have established your short- and long-term goals, it will also be important to prioritize each one. Here, ask yourself which goals are the most important. As an example, if reaching a certain amount of savings is a key goal, then before doing anything else, you should earmark a certain amount of your income each month to go into your employer-sponsored retirement plan, an IRA, and / or other savings or investment accounts.

Having a clear vision will help you to be more confident about setting - and successfully achieving - your retirement destination. In addition, having this clarity can also help to reduce any anxiety that you may have about taking that important step away from relying on your employer for income and towards relying on yourself.

Programming your goals into your GPS can provide you with a specific track to run on, and it will let you know if or when you have gone off course. This can make it much easier to re-route so that your goals can be accomplished, rather than waiting until it is too late.

Chapter 3: Leaving a Legacy

We all want to be remembered. As we move through life, many people start to think about what is truly important - not just from a financial standpoint, but from an emotional one as well.

Certainly, for those who have substantial financial means, there is the possibility of providing large charitable donations to organizations that have meaning to you, in return for recognition. But, in the case of many people, leaving a legacy can actually mean much more than just money.

It also does not necessarily require that you do big things or that you complete major accomplishments in order to leave a legacy. Oftentimes, being remembered has much more to do with how you have lived your life as versus achieving world-renown feats.

Establishing Your Specific Purpose

It typically goes without saying that those who do not have adequate financial means would be much happier if they had more money to be able to have and do the things that they want. Yet, while your wealth and income can tend to increase your overall well-being, there are some other key factors that also matter.

In fact, according to an economics expert at the University of Aberdeen, there are two other primary criteria that can have an even larger effect on your overall fulfillment in retirement than just money alone. These include your health, and the reason for your retiring. In other words, whether or not you have a purpose.

Many people may not initially realize what an adjustment it can be adapting to a new routine - even if that routine doesn't involve setting an alarm clock and sitting in traffic every week on the way to and from a job.

According to the research director at the Sloan Center on Aging & Work at Boston College, there is actual data that shows there is a type of "honeymoon" period in retirement at the beginning. Here, it may feel like you are on vacation or you have a new-found freedom.

But, after that, there can oftentimes be another period of time when people begin to realize that this is how it will be for the rest of their lives - and in some cases, it isn't enough. This is why is it so incredibly important to have a clear cut purpose for what you will do with your time in the future.

But, not only can having a clear cut purpose help you with being happier overall - and make your retirement more fulfilling - in many instances, it can also help you to live a longer life. In fact, David Buettner, a writer and explorer, has spent the bulk of his life traveling the world in search of answers.

In his 2008 book titled "The Blue Zones: Lessons for Living Longer From the People Who've Lived the Longest," Buettner interviewed centenarians from around the world in order to determine why they thought they had lived so long. What he discovered was that, in every culture that he studied, there was a notion of ikigai - which means having a reason to get up in the morning and having a purpose.

Buettner also found that people are the happiest when they spend their time and money on experiences, as versus on objects. With that in mind, taking up an interest in the arts, sports, or any other activity that you enjoy will provide longer term satisfaction than any one purchase of a "thing". For example, learning to play a new musical instrument or learning a new language can essentially pay "dividends" for many years to come.[1]

A purpose in retirement can also be more intellectually stimulating. While you don't need to work at your purpose 24 / 7, there can be enormous advantages to knowing your next direction. And, depending on what you ultimately decide to do, you may also be able to enhance your financial well-being.

For example, by working on a part-time basis or setting up a new business, you don't have to forge ahead at 50 or 60-hour weeks. Rather, take it easy, enjoy what you are doing, and reap the benefits of that.

Leveraging Your Options

Legacies take many forms, though perhaps the most common legacy is a lifetime gift or a bequest of cash. When we think of cash legacies, we tend to think in terms of what the very rich can afford to give away because this is what makes the evening news. This can sometimes make our own efforts appear insignificant by comparison, but this doesn't have to be the case.

It's possible to leverage small gifts to generate a much larger, more powerful monetary legacy, in just the same way that contributing small annual contributions to a retirement plan accumulate to become a significant source of retirement income. In the realm of legacy building, while far from being the only way to leave a monetary legacy, the most common vehicle employed is a life insurance policy.

With life insurance, small annual premium payments can guarantee much more opportunity to an individual or organization you want to leave a legacy than would be possible otherwise. And this is the point: expanded opportunity, opportunity that can be guaranteed to someone for whom you want to provide the means to have the best and deepest life experience or guaranteed financial security, or to an organization that promotes the kind of good work in the world you want to see done.

And this kind of legacy planning can be accomplished without jeopardizing your own long-term financial security.[2]

How to Ensure That Your Legacy Will Live On

Your purpose in life can also move you towards leaving your desired legacy. For some people, the end goal of paying off your debts and saving money for a secure retirement may be enough. But in order to truly have a successful retirement, it should include ensuring that you have not only taken care of yourself, but that you've also taken care of others. That may encompass your spouse, your children, and other loved ones, as well as other people and / or entities that you care about.

Unfortunately, only 56% of American retirees actually plan to leave an inheritance for their children. One reason for this is because most believe that they won't have any money left to leave after they have made it through retirement.[3]

But, by following a carefully crafted financial plan that works for you, you can end up leaving a legacy - both of love and financial means. And, doing so can not only affect your immediate descendants, but many generations to come.

In order to ensure that this occurs, though, it will be important that you map out not just getting to - and through - your retirement years, but also chart a course for what will happen afterwards. And, just as with any other type of successful plan of action, what I have found in my nearly 30 years of experience, is that this will entail a course that is specific to you.

Sources

1. "How to 'Thrive': Dan Buettner's Secrets of Happiness." NPR Books. (http://www.npr.org/2010/11/28/131571885/how-to-thrive-dan-buettner-s-secrets-of-happiness)

2. Estate, Business and Retirement Planning Specialist, Les Von Losberg.

3. "What Financial Legacy are You Leaving Behind?" Chris Hogan. (https://www.chrishogan360.com/what-financial-legacy-are-you-leaving-behind/)

Chapter 4: Where Do You Want to Live?

Throughout the years, you may have dreamed about living by the beach, in the mountains, or being close to family and friends who currently reside far away. It can be fun to think about where you might be in the future. But in order to make it a reality, it is important that you first nail down some key factors that are involved in the process.

For example, while you may want to downsize your current living situation and / or move to a different part of the country, actually doing so can be a major endeavor. That's why having a plan in place can make it that much easier when the time comes.

Should You Stay or Go? Considerations Around Moving in Retirement

The first consideration is determining where you will reside. Do you want to remain in your current home, or is another area of the country - or even another country altogether - more appealing to you?

In some cases, people will pick up and move to a warmer climate or other location of choice without really giving it much thought. Unfortunately, this could turn out to be an expensive mistake.

So, before moving forward with a major move - especially one that may be hundreds or thousands of miles away from your current locale - be sure to consider the following:

- **Living Costs** - The cost of living in another locale could be drastically different from where you currently reside. So, be sure that you have a good idea regarding what your ongoing expenses will be (on top of the cost of actually moving).

- **Lifestyle** - The things to do that affect your overall lifestyle can also differ in other locations. While you may have even vacationed in your chosen spot, living somewhere on a permanent basis can be another story altogether. For example, relaxing on the beach every day may at first sound ideal. But, on a permanent basis, this could become mundane.

- **Support System** - Ensuring that you have a good support system is also a key factor. Here, will you be moving closer or farther away from family and friends? If it's the latter, will you have someone to call in your new location in case of an emergency? And what about social activities on a regular basis?

- **Health** - In determining an out-of-town move, you should also factor in your current, and your anticipated future health. In your new location, will you still have access to doctors and other medical facilities that you may need?

- **Marital Status** - Your marital status can also play a primary role in where you end up living. This is especially the case if you are married and your spouse is still working. If you do move, will he or she also quit their job or retire, or will they need to find a new place of employment in your new location? So this, too, is something that will need to be worked out.

If you do opt to make a move to another city, state, or country, it can help if you initially rent your housing there for at least the first 6 to 12 months. This can allow you the opportunity to get a feel for what the area is like on a full-time basis, yet without investing a large chunk of money in a home that you'll need to soon sell if you find that you don't really want to live there.

When making your actual move, you will also need to determine the logistics. For example, what will you be taking with you? Will you need to sell or donate some (or all) of your current furniture and other household items before you go?

Will you need to hire a moving company, or will friends and family help out with the heavy lifting and transporting of your items? And, if you do need to use a professional mover - especially for a long-distance trip - you will need to do some research on the companies that you are considering, as well as obtain more than just one bid.

Types of Housing

Once you have determined what area you want to reside in, the next key factor in the process is deciding in what type of housing you will live. If you have opted to remain in your present area, staying in your current home is certainly an option.

This can often be a good choice if the size of your home is manageable, and you have friends in the neighborhood. It can also work out well if your home is paid for and / or the expenses fit nicely into your budget.

If you decide that your current home may not be the best option for you, then you could consider alternate living arrangements, such as a:

- **Condo or Apartment** - Moving to a condo or an apartment can offer many advantages - starting with the fact that most (or all) of your maintenance will be taken care of by someone else. Not only can this free up more of your time to travel or do other activities that you enjoy, but it can also mean that you won't be required to perform various tasks that could be strenuous.

- **Retirement Community** - A retirement community can also be another potential option. Today, retirement communities can offer a lot of wonderful amenities as well as conveniences. In addition to having your maintenance issues taken care of, there are many retirement communities that offer prepared meals, on-site beauty shops and barbers, and a wide array of social activities to choose from. Depending on the type of community that you choose, there may even be the option to receive healthcare and / or long-term nursing care if it should be required in the future.

Expenses to Consider

Other than healthcare, one of the biggest expenses that you can face in retirement is your housing. Regardless of whether you rent or own your residence, you will typically still need to allocate a certain amount of your retirement income to go towards your housing related costs. These can include the following:

- Rent or Mortgage Payment
- Utilities (such as natural gas, electric, water, sewer, and trash)
- Maintenance and Upkeep
- Insurance
- Property Taxes (if applicable)

Alternatively, if you decide to go the route of a retirement community, you may have all of these expenses rolled into just one, single convenient monthly payment. And, in some cases, there may also be an up-front deposit that you'll be required to make.

The Many Options for Retirement Living

There are many possible living options that may be available to you in retirement. So, in order to ensure that you make the best decision for you, be sure that you do an ample amount of research on them all - even if you have been leaning in a particular direction for a long time. That way, you will have all of the potential pros and cons fresh in your mind so that you can move forward with confidence.

Chapter 5: What Do You Want to Do When You Retire?

Preparing for retirement can be exciting. As you get closer to that point in your life and your finances, it means that the time you have been dreaming about for many years can finally be coming into reality. But, in order to have the successful retirement that you've been imagining, it is essential that you have a good plan.

When you have a plan - more specifically, one that includes your goals - it can help you to make more accurate decisions with regard to how you are going to get there. Without this, you could be flying blind.

For instance, imagine looking at your vehicle's GPS system and asking it how to get somewhere - but without adding in an actual destination. No matter how high-tech your system is, if you don't tell it where you want to go, the directions on how to get there can be pretty inaccurate.

Unfortunately, many people "plan" for retirement this way, with no clear cut destination. For example, they may put money into a 401(k) every month, and possibly even have some personal savings and investments.

But, just randomly saving money or investing without an ending point can still lead these investors down an inaccurate path. Then, when the time for retirement comes, they may find that they don't have enough income to provide for the living expenses that they'll need in order to enjoy their intended lifestyle.

This isn't necessarily the fault to the investor, though. For example, even though many companies offer 401(k)s or other types of retirement savings options, these plans don't usually come with a set of instructions on how to properly allocate those funds.

Likewise, there are also some financial professionals who may be more willing to sell you the "investment of the day" rather than putting together an actual financial plan that is incorporated with your goals. But, before you invest in anything for retirement, it is absolutely essential that you first know where you want to be and what you want to do when you get there.

How to Determine What You Really Want to Do When You Retire

Although a long-term vacation might seem nice, it can actually be quite difficult to walk away from doing something that you've been doing for many years. In addition, there also comes a social and emotional aspect to your work life, which can be tough to leave behind.

With that in mind, it is important to ensure that you are emotionally ready to retire. In going about this, you should begin to determine what you will do in order to keep yourself challenged and engaged after you say goodbye to your co-workers.

The question of what to do in retirement is actually more important than many people might think. Most may say that they would like to have a nice mix of travel, relaxation, and fun once they leave the world of employment, although there are some people - more, in fact, every year - who also would like to participate in more meaningful work in the future.

As far as the actual specifics go, though, the activities that you want to engage in may not be quite as pinpointed. So, in order to have a truly successful retirement, determining how you will spend your time can be equally as important as the financial aspect.

How exactly do you determine what you really want to do when you retire?

In some cases, you may already have a burning desire to accomplish certain goals or to participate in specific activities. For instance, you might know that you've always wanted to hike in all the U.S. mountain ranges, or visit the top 20 golf courses in the world.

Alternatively, you may have a heartfelt desire to spend your time volunteering with a favorite charity, tutor students who need extra help with certain course work, write the next big bestselling novel, or start a brand new online business.

But, if you are still struggling with what it is that you truly want to spend the next phase of your life doing, there are some questions that you can ask yourself in order to get you started down the right path.

These include:

- What are your key ideals and / or priorities?
- If you were to pass away tomorrow, what would be your top 5 biggest regrets?
- If you were able to start your life over - but already knowing all that you know right now - what, if anything, would you do differently?
- Who in this world matters the most to you, and likewise, who are you important to?
- When you reflect back on your life, what were you the happiest doing - and why?
- What are some activities and / or hobbies that you enjoy doing?
- If you could stop doing anything in your life, what would those things include?
- What are your key skills and talents?
- If someone asked you why you want to retire, what would your answer be?

You can also help to narrow down what you want to do in retirement with the help of some online resources. For instance, AARP offers a variety of tools and exercises that can assist you with sparking some ideas, and you don't have to be a member of AARP in order to use them. With its "Life Reimagined" program, you can better visualize your future by using the LifeMap, and you can even sign up to work with a life coach who can help you to focus and solidify your next steps.

In addition, it can be helpful to pin down where it is that you want to live, as well as whether or not there is anyone else who will depending on you for income in the future. In answering these questions, it will help to tie together both the financial and the emotional aspects of setting your retirement goals.

Could You or Should You Continue to Work in Retirement?

Even if you can financially afford to retire, there are some people who may opt to keep on working. This work may be continued at a current job, or it may entail doing something completely different - but that you have always wanted to do.

By continuing to receive a paycheck - even for just a few more years - you will likely be able to improve your retirement finances by adding to your savings, which can in turn, be used to generate future income.

If you do decide to continue working, though - or to start a new money making endeavor - there are some key factors that you should consider in order to determine whether or not you should pursue a particular option.

For instance, in some cases, if you will also be drawing on your Social Security retirement benefits, you could end up putting yourself in a position where the benefits will be taxed. Depending on how much you make each year, as well as your age, and the way that you file your tax return, up to 85% of your Social Security income could be taxed when you earn income from wages and certain other sources, including:

- Self-employment income
- Interest
- Dividends
- Other income that must be reported on your taxes

In addition, depending on the total amount of your earnings each year, you may also run the risk of putting yourself into a higher income tax bracket. This may not only cause you to pay more to Uncle Sam, but it could have other adverse effects, as well, such as increasing the amount that you pay for your annual Medicare Part B premium.

Finding the Perfect Fit

If you decide that going forward with a job (full- or part-time) is your ideal direction, then it will be important that you find the perfect fit. Provided that you don't already have a particular job in mind, you could do some research, based on how you would ideally like to spend your time.

You can also seek out various job ideas by visiting websites like Workforce50.org and RetirementJobs.org. These sites literally list thousands of jobs from coast to coast from companies that are actively seeking older workers.

If you prefer freelance or work-from-home opportunities, there are resources for that, as well, such as FlexJobs.com, Upwork.com, and Guru.com. Going this route can allow you to earn an income on your own time and terms, while at the same time, providing you with the flexibility to travel, relax, or participate in other activities when you're not "on the clock."

Considering the Whole Picture Prior to Moving Forward

By incorporating the GPS method, you will start with a "top down" approach. This initially takes a look at the big picture overall. Then, it breaks down your intentions into more specific strategies that can be used for getting you where you want to go.

Using the GPS system, you will also be able to determine whether you have various "gaps" in your current plan or savings program. Such gaps may otherwise have gone unnoticed if you did not have a specific projection for getting you to your intended future goals. With the GPS method, though, not only will you be able to pick out the gaps, but the strategies that you use will help you to fill those gaps in.

One of the most important components of using the GPS method is ensuring that you do not wait until it's too late to put your plan in motion. For example, sometimes, when you are traveling to an uncharted destination, you may find that you're on the wrong road. If you catch the mistake in time, it can be easier to turn around and get back on the right track.

In other instances, though, regardless of how hard you may try, if the error is realized too late, the chances are that you aren't going to get to your destination - at least not without having to make some significant revisions to your plan that could end up getting you to your end goal much later than you had initially hoped. With that in mind, there is no better time than right now to determine what you want to do, and then start implementing the plan that will allow you to do that.

Chapter 6: How Much Will Your Retirement Lifestyle *Really* Cost?

In planning to have enough income in retirement - both in terms of being able to pay your monthly living expenses, and ensuring that your income will last as long as you need it to - it is essential to plan beyond just the immediate time frame that you leave the work force.

And, while providing a way to account for inflation can be a good start, that alone may not be enough. This is because your actual income needs can change - sometimes drastically - throughout the course of your retirement years.

There are many financial planners who may estimate that retirees will require 70% or 80% of their pre-retirement earnings in order to maintain their current lifestyle in retirement. In some instances, this may be a starting point.

However, just simply applying a generic income replacement rate such as that, across the board, for the entire time period that you may be retired is not the proper way to determine what a retiree will *really* need - either at the beginning of the retirement journey, and especially throughout the many years that your retirement could last.

Estimating Your True Expenses in Retirement

Although you may be saving money for retirement, and you might even have a good idea of what your living expenses will be at that time, it is also important to take an additional step in the retirement income planning process - and that is to attribute for the fact that your expenses will likely change over time. This is especially the case when planning for longer retirement terms like 20 or 30 years.

Think about it for a moment. Are your expenses today the same as they were 20 years ago - even setting aside the inflation factor? In most situations, living expenses will change over the course of many years in order to account for your different needs.

With that in mind, you may be able to project an approximate figure for what your monthly obligations will be at the beginning of your retirement years. But, in order to have a truly successful income plan, it will take a deeper dive.

Spending Trends in Retirement

It has been said that, "the only constant is change." This is true throughout your life, and it will continue to be true as you make your way through the many years that you may spend in retirement.

The good news here is that, in many cases, while you may be planning for income that will help you to maintain certain lifestyle needs, the amount of real income that you need may actually decrease as time goes on.

Based on research from a study titled, "Estimating the True Cost of Retirement," put out by Morningstar, real retiree spending actually decreases, on average, slowly during the early retirement years.

According to the study, these early years of retirement are termed as the "Go-Go Years," because this is the time when retirees are initially enjoying their new-found time freedom. In most cases, this is also the time when you will be the healthiest, and in turn, able to live an active lifestyle.

As individuals move through the spectrum of their retirement years, though, they will reach a new phase, aptly termed by the Morningstar study as the "Slow-Go" years. Here, as health and energy start to decline, spending will too.

In the "Slow-Go" phase, retirees will typically begin to slow down with activities like travel and eating out, which account for a bulk of their discretionary expenses, and accordingly, spending at this point will oftentimes decline more rapidly. Retirees who are considered more affluent can really see a difference here.

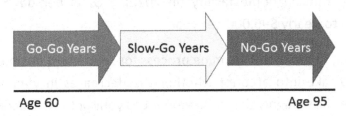

Source: Estimating Changes In Retirement Expenditures and the Retirement Spending Smile. Nerd's Eye View at Kitces.com. April 30, 2014.

Then, as retirees move into the third and final phase of retirement, which is referred to in the study as the "No-Go" years, spending will continue to decrease, but it will do so more slowly than in the prior phase.[1]

During the time period of the "No-Go" years, many retirees may even see an almost total shut down of activity-related spending, as consumption decreases to just the primary expenses that are needed to maintain the household.[2]

Are You Leaving Anything Out?

While many retirees may see a dip in real expenses over time, as your spending on activity and travel may be decreasing, there is another potential expense that might be looming - and this one has the ability to literally decimate your whole portfolio if it isn't properly planned for. This is the cost of health care - and more specifically, the cost of a long-term care need.

According to Genworth's Cost of Care Survey 2016, long-term care can cost a lot - and on average, the price tag for a private room in a skilled nursing home facility (in 2016) is $263 per day.[3] This equates to nearly $96,000 per year!

With that in mind, the planning process for retirement income will need to take into account whether the decreases in your living expenses are roughly the same amount as your potential increases in spending for medical and long-term care.

According to further research conducted by David Blanchett, CFA, CFP, who is the Head of Retirement Research at Morningstar, many retirees' spending needs will start at a certain point, then dip as activities slow down, and then rise again when more income is needed for healthcare. When tracked on a graph, this change in consumption patterns will actually resemble a smile.

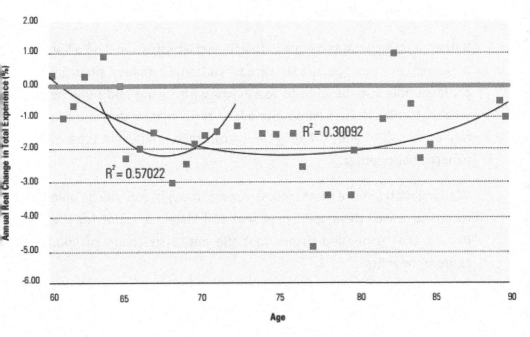

The Retirement Spending Smile

Source: Estimating Changes In Retirement Expenditures and the Retirement Spending Smile. Nerd's Eye View at Kitces.com. April 30, 2014.

The Real Cost of Your Retirement Lifestyle

Just as you travel on a journey, your vehicle will not move forward at the exact same rate of speed the entire time. The same can be said for the amount of income that you will need over the full course of your retirement years.

That being said, the reality is that the real cost of your retirement needs will also be highly personalized, based on your specific facts and circumstances. This is why planning for retirement income is not a do-it-yourself endeavor.

Rather, it is important to work with a financial professional who has a focus in this particular area. Although many financial professionals may be able to assist you with saving and building wealth, turning those savings into a long-term income that you can rely on for all of your ongoing needs can take a different type of expertise altogether.

Working with a retirement income expert, though, you will be able to create a well-developed plan that will ideally account for the income that is needed throughout the entire spectrum of your retirement years.

Sources

1. Estimating Changes In Retirement Expenditures and the Retirement Spending Smile. Nerd's Eye View at Kitces.com. April 30, 2014.

2. Ibid.

3. Cost of Care Survey 2016. Genworth. (https://www.genworth.com/dam/Americas/US/PDFs/Consumer/corporate/131168_050516.pdf)

Chapter 7: Income Sources in Retirement

Knowing if you will be able to retire soon can take piecing together all of your potential income sources and then determining whether you will have enough to see you through what could be a 20 or 30 year time period.

Traditionally, income in retirement had come from three primary sources. These include Social Security, pensions, and personal savings or investments. These three income sources have been referred to as the "three legged stool."

But today's - and tomorrow's - retirement has changed a great deal from the way that it was even just a few decades ago. For instance, there is a fair amount of uncertainty with Social Security. Plus, people are saving less for their futures, and pension plans are literally disappearing.

In addition, while traditional retirement income sources have become less reliable (or have vanished altogether), people are living longer lives today. This means that the income that you will have in retirement will need to last for a much longer period of time than it did in generations past.

In fact, based on a study by LIMRA, a worldwide association of insurance and financial services firms, half of retiree couples are likely to have one spouse who will live to age 90. And, one in four may even have one spouse who will live to be 94.[1]

The study further concluded that, with excellent health status, one quarter of retirees could live to age 97, and in one out of eight retiree couples, either one or both of the spouses will live to celebrate their 100th birthday.[2]

So, because of your odds for living in retirement for a long period of time, it is essential that you not only make the most of your income sources, but that you are able to coordinate them so as to net you the most beneficial result.

Where Will Your Retirement Income Come From?

There is a wide variety of sources from which you may be able to receive your income in retirement. Each of these may be treated a little differently with regard to your deposits, as well as taxes - both going into the account, and coming out.

Your retirement income sources may include some (or all) of the following:

Pension

In the past, if you worked for a big company, chances are that you were covered by the company's pension plan. These retirement income sources, officially known as defined benefit pension plans, had a number of nice advantages - starting with the fact that retirees could oftentimes receive income for the rest of their lives, regardless of how long that may be. These plans would also typically pay out at least some amount of ongoing income to the surviving spouse when the retired employee passed away.

In addition, it was up to the company - not the retired employee - to compensate for any investment losses, so that the individual would still be able to receive the set amount of ongoing income that they were promised. In many instances, the employee was not even responsible for making any contributions from their wages into the plan.

Unfortunately, due in large part to the high expense of keeping these plans in force, most companies have stopped offering defined benefit pension plans, and have replaced them with defined contribution plans.

In a defined contribution plan, as the name suggests, the contribution into the plan is the factor that is known, as versus the amount of income that the plan pays out. The most popular of the defined contribution plans today is the 401(k).

401(k)

You may have access to a 401(k) plan through your employer. If so, these plans can offer you the opportunity to invest for retirement in a tax-deferred manner. This means that the investment gains that take place inside of your 401(k) plan can be deferred until the time they are withdrawn.

This can allow for the account to grow and compound exponentially, because not only are you receiving gains on top of gains, but also growth on the amount of money that *would have otherwise been* taken out in taxes.

You can also typically make your 401(k) plan contributions with pre-tax dollars. That means that the amount of your contribution does not have to be counted in your income on your tax return - in turn, allowing you to pay less in income tax for that year. That's the good news.

The other side of the 401(k) plan "coin" is that, unlike a defined benefit pension plan, where you know how much income you can count on in retirement, participants in a 401(k) plan must take care of converting the funds over to income on their own. This can mean that you may - or may not - have enough income generated from this plan in order to cover your living expenses in retirement.

Adding to that, 401(k) plan participants must also be careful of market downturns - which could essentially wipe out all of the gains, and even the principal, during a negative period. And, if you are close to retirement age, you may not have enough time to build your account balance back up.

The majority of the money that is deposited into a 401(k) plan will come from the employee - although the employer may offer a "matching" contribution. In addition, 401(k) plans are capped at how much a participant can put in each year.

For example, in 2016, if you are age 49 or younger, you can defer up to $18,000 into your plan, and if you are age 50 or older, you can defer an additional $6,000 in what is referred to as "catch up" contribution.

Unfortunately, 401(k) plans do not often come with instruction manuals. While your employer may provide some guidance in terms of brochures or other marketing material, for the most part, employees are oftentimes unsure about how to best allocate the funds that are inside of their 401(k) plan. This can sometimes lead to investment losses and / or lack of properly invested funds.

Sources

1. The Retirement Income Reference Book. LIMRA. Page 78. Copyright 2012.

2. Ibid.

Chapter 8: Income in Retirement from IRAs (Individual Retirement Accounts)

Many investors may take advantage of the tax benefits that are allowed when investing in Individual Retirement Accounts, or IRAs. These types of accounts can allow you various tax benefits on your contributions, your withdrawals, and / or on the taxation (or lack of) on the growth that takes place inside of the account, depending on which type of IRA account you have.

There are two types of IRA accounts available. These include the Traditional and the Roth option:

Traditional IRA Account

With a Traditional IRA, you can typically deduct some or all of your annual contribution. This means that the amount that you contribute into your account will not have to be counted as income for that year. This essentially means that you will pay less in income tax for the year.

The growth that takes place inside of a Traditional IRA is tax-deferred, which means that you also won't be required to pay taxes on your Traditional IRA funds until the time they are withdrawn in the future. For many people, your income tax bracket in retirement may be less than it is during your working years. This, too, can be beneficial, as you could end up paying less in tax overall.

In 2016, you are allowed to contribute up to $5,500 to a Traditional IRA if you are age 49 or younger. If you are age 50 or older, you can contribute an additional $1,000 in "catch up" contribution amount. The amount of this contribution that can be deducted will be dependent on how much you earn, as well as whether or not you are a participant in a retirement plan through your employer.

You can, however, "rollover" funds into an IRA from a 401(k) or other qualifying type of retirement account. For example, if you are rolling funds from your employer-sponsored 401(k) into a Traditional IRA account upon retirement, there are no dollar maximums for going this route.

This can really help to increase the amount of money that you have in your IRA for generating retirement income. It can also give you a lot more control over what you are able to invest in. For example, many 401(k) plans will only provide you with a list of certain mutual funds and other investments that you are allowed to invest in.

But with an IRA account, you have a wide variety of stocks, bonds, mutual funds, and other investments that you can invest your funds into. So, if you have left any 401(k) funds with a former employer, it can be extremely beneficial for you to roll those funds over into your own personal IRA.

Roth IRA Account

With a Roth IRA, you won't be able to deduct your contributions on your annual tax return. However, not only will the funds that are inside of the account be allowed to grow tax-free, but you can also withdraw your funds from a Roth IRA tax-free in retirement.

The maximum amount that you are allowed to deposit into a Roth IRA is the same as that of a Traditional IRA. Be aware, though, that you cannot deposit $5,500 (or $6,500, if age 50 or over) into BOTH types of IRA accounts each year.

Rather, there are annual maximum limits on IRA contributions across the board. So, for example, if you are age 50 or over in 2016, you can essentially have both a Traditional and a Roth IRA – but you can only deposit a maximum of $6,500 in total between the two.

In order to participate in a Roth IRA account, your annual income will be taken into consideration. The limitation will be dependent on how much you earn, as well as how you file your annual tax return. The figures for 2016 are:

2016 Income Limitations / Requirements

Roth IRA Income Limits for Single Tax Filers	Phase-out starts at $117,000 Ineligible to contribute at $132,000 or over
Roth IRA Income Limits for Married Tax Filers	Phase-out starts at $184,000 Ineligible to contribute at $194,000

Source: IRS.gov

While you may be planning to retire early, it is important to keep in mind both the taxes that you may have to pay, as well as whether or not you will be required to pay an IRS (Internal Revenue Service) "early withdrawal" penalty.

For instance, just as with an employer-sponsored 401(k) or other retirement plan, you may be required to pay 10% - in addition to any taxes that are due – if you take money out of your IRA account before you reach the age of 59 ½.

It will also be essential to be mindful of whether or not you are required to withdraw money from your IRA when you reach a certain age. For instance, with a Traditional IRA, based on the Required Minimum Distribution (RMD) rules, you will be required to begin taking out at least a minimum amount of money by the April 1st of the year after you turn age 70 ½.

In order to receive your Required Minimum Distribution from your Traditional IRA, you can either make a one-time lump-sum withdrawal, or alternatively, you can take a series of annual withdrawals. It is extremely important to keep the RMD rules in mind, as not taking your required withdrawal for the year – or not taking enough of a withdrawal – can result in penalties from the IRS.

Social Security

Although we have heard a fair amount of news over the past decade or so about the instability of the Social Security program, the reality is that you are likely to still receive income from Social Security in retirement.

In fact, more than 65 million people currently receive some type of benefits from Social Security, and in the year 2015, there were approximately 5.4 people who were newly awarded Social Security benefits.(1)

It is important to note, though, that even if you do receive retirement income benefits from Social Security, they may not be enough to meet your lifestyle requirements - or even to pay all of your living expenses when you retire.

This is because, according to the Social Security Administration itself, "[But] Social Security was never meant to be the only source of income for people when they retire. Social Security replaces about 40 percent of an average wage earner's income after retiring, and most financial advisors say a retiree will need 70 percent or more of pre-retirement earnings to live comfortably." (2)

With that in mind, while you will likely receive some amount of income from Social Security in retirement, it is important to have other sources of income, too, so that you won't have to rely on just this one income stream.

Investments

Many retirees may also receive income from the personal savings and investments that they have accumulated throughout the years. Some of these sources may include CDs, bonds, treasury notes, interest and / or dividends, as well as retirement annuities.

Over the years, many financial advisors have used "draw down" strategies that consist of taking a certain amount of income from a retiree's portfolio, while leaving the remainder of the funds inside of the portfolio to continue growing.

One popular retirement income drawdown method is referred to as the "4 Percent Rule." Using this particular strategy, 4% of your over overall portfolio would be withdrawn as income, leaving the rest of your money to continue growing.

However, due in large part to the volatile stock market of today, along with a historically low interest rate environment over the past several years, the 4% rule has actually come under some scrutiny, as it could end up depleting the portfolio more quickly than in years gone by – this can be especially detrimental if this is the only source of retirement income that you have.

In addition, this strategy may or may not be able to provide the increasing amount of income that you would need in order to keep up with the rising cost of goods and services – due to inflation - that you would have to keep purchasing over time.

By knowing how much you may need for expenses in retirement, it can be much easier to plan going forward. You may also be able to determine where any "gaps" lie between what you will need and what you will have. Being able to plan for those gaps now, as versus after you've retired, can make your desired retirement lifestyle more possible to accomplish.

Sources

"Understanding the Benefits." Social Security. 2016.
(https://www.ssa.gov/pubs/EN-05-10024.pdf)

Fast Facts & Figures About Social Security, 2016.
(https://www.ssa.gov/policy/docs/chartbooks/fast_facts/2016/fa
st_facts16.html#pagei)

Chapter 9: Income Sources in Retirement – Annuities and Wages

One income source that has become increasingly popular with retirees is annuities. This is because an annuity can provide you with an income stream for the remainder of your life - regardless of how long that may be. So, having this type of financial vehicle can truly help to ease the concern of running out of income in retirement.

Not all annuities are the same, though, so if you plan to purchase one, it is absolutely essential that you have an understanding of how it works, and even more so, how it will work for you and your specific needs based on your future income requirements, your risk tolerance, and your anticipated time horizon.

First, an annuity can be either immediate or deferred. An immediate annuity can allow you to start receiving income immediately - or very soon after you purchase it. The income payments that you receive will be based on several factors, including the amount that you deposit (which, with immediate annuities, is just one lump sum from your personal savings or that is "rolled over" from a retirement plan such as an IRA or 401(k)). It will also be based on your anticipated life expectancy.

Alternatively, deferred annuities pay out income at some time in the future. With these types of annuities, you can either make just one lump sum deposit, or you can make many deposits over time, until you are ready to convert the money in the account over to an income stream.

There are several different types of deferred annuities that you may choose from. These include:

- Fixed Annuities - During their "accumulation" phase, a fixed annuity will offer you a set amount of interest that is credited annually from the insurance company that you purchased it through. When the time comes to convert the annuity's funds into income - referred to as "annuitizing" - you will be able to choose from several different payout options. While they typically offer a lower return, one of the primary benefits with fixed annuities is the safety of principal that they offer, along with knowing that you will have a set amount of regular income when you need it.

- Variable Annuities - During the accumulation period with a variable annuity, you have the opportunity to participate in market appreciation through a number of different investment options. Here, you won't invest directly in the market, but rather in "sub-accounts" that include equities like mutual funds. Although variable annuities may be able to attain a nice return during market upswings, you can also be exposed to the risk of a downturn in the market as well.

- Fixed Index Annuities - In an index annuity, your return in the account will be linked to an external equity index, such as the S&P 500. Here, you have the ability to attain a nice market index-based return - up to a certain cap. In return for that, though, your funds are also protected from market downturns. For example, typically, if the index that the annuity is tracking has negative performance in a given year, the account will simply be credited with a 0% for that time period. So, while you don't gain at that time, you also don't lose.

In addition to the income stream that they can provide, annuities can also offer some nice advantages while you are still in your working and saving years. One key benefit is that, unlike IRAs and employer-sponsored retirement plans, there is no maximum annual contribution for non-qualified annuities.

So, if you have already "maxed out" your tax-advantaged retirement plan contributions for the year, an annuity can provide you with the ability to obtain additional tax-deferred savings for the future. In addition, you may also be able to start withdrawing money from a non-qualified annuity without incurring a 10% IRS "early withdrawal" penalty if you are younger than age 59 1/2.

Wages

Another component of your retirement income may actually include wages from a job. In fact, continued employment - whether it is in the same or a different field - has become a much more common aspect today. According to Bloomberg, due to the substantial number of Baby Boomers who are now age 65 and over, there are a record number of retirees who are choosing to remain in the workforce.

The latest Bloomberg figures show that approximately 19% of older Americans are working, which is the highest number since the early 1960s. This, however, could be both a positive and a negative, depending on what the reason is for continuing (or going back) to work.

For example, in some cases, people will retire from their full-time job and move on to another part-time or freelance endeavor because it is something that they've always wanted to do. In other cases, though, individuals are reaching retirement age and realizing that they have an income "gap" - more expenses each month than income - and they find that they have to work in order to pay the bills.

If you do opt to remain or go back into the workforce in retirement, there are some positive trends taking place. For instance, due to a relatively tight labor market today, there are many employers that are increasingly relying on skilled older workers.

There are also some potential benefits for you if you remain actively working. First, remaining physically and socially active can keep you healthier, and in turn, happier. Continued income could also mean that you can set some more money aside for when you are ready to fully retire and live off of your investments.

One word of caution, though, is that if you are already taking retirement benefits from Social Security, you could end up having at least a portion of those benefits taxed if you earn "too much."

For example, if you are under your full retirement age and you are taking your retirement benefits from Social Security, you could be required to pay income tax on up to 85% of your benefit, depending on your filing status and the amount that you earn.

In 2016, if you file a federal tax return as an individual, and your combined income is:

- Between $25,000 and $34,000, then you may have to pay income tax on up to 50% of your benefits
- More than $34,000, then up to 85% of your benefits may be taxed.

If you file a joint income tax return, and you and your spouse have a combined income that is:

- Between $32,000 and $44,000, then you may be required to pay income tax on up to 50% of your Social Security benefits
- More than $44,000, up to 85% of your benefits may be taxable.

If you are married and you file a separate tax return, then you will also likely need to pay tax on at least a portion of your Social Security retirement benefits.[1]

Note that when Social Security refers to "combined income", this means your adjusted gross income, plus your non-taxable interest that is received, plus half of your Social Security benefits.[2]

Should you have the ability and the option to work in retirement, this could also mean that you are one of the lucky ones. That's because, according to the Employee Benefit Research Institute, roughly half of retirees left the workforce earlier than expected in 2015. Some of the reasons for that included employer downsizing, health issues of the employee, and / or the need for an employee to care for a loved one.

With that in mind, finding a new job or remaining in the working world can offer some advantages. But, if you are counting on this avenue to help you with shoring up your nest egg, it may not necessarily pan out. So, it is essential to have a good, solid retirement income plan in place too...just in case.

Sources

1. Social Security Administration. www.ssa.gov.

2. Ibid.

Chapter 10: Tax Considerations in Retirement

Taxes are a concept that most of us have to deal with throughout our entire lives - and, when you reach retirement, taxes usually don't stop. This includes being taxed on the things that you buy, as well as receiving income that may be taxed. So, there are several tax-related considerations that you can face in retirement.

There can also be several misconceptions when it comes to taxes in retirement. For instance, many financial professionals will tell you that you will be in a lower income tax bracket in retirement. But, this is not necessarily true.

Depending on the amount of your income, you will currently fall into one of seven different tax brackets. Knowing which one you fall into is the first step to understanding what percentage of your income you must give to Uncle Sam.

2016 Income Tax Brackets

Rate	Single Filers	Married Filing Jointly	Head of Household
10%	$0 to $9,275	$0 to $18,550	$0 to $13,250
15%	$9,275 to $37,650	$18,550 to $75,300	$13,250 to $50,400
25%	$37,650 to $91,150	$75,300 to $151,900	$50,400 to $130,150
28%	$91,150 to $190,150	$151,900 to $231,450	$130,150 to $210,800
33%	$190,150 to $413,350	$231,450 to $413,350	$210,800 to $413,350
35%	$413,350 to $415,050	$413,350 to $466,950	$413,350 to $441,000
39.6%	$415,050+	$466,950+	$441,000+

Source: www.IRS.gov

So, in using 2016 figures, the lowest tax bracket for single people requires that you earn $9,275 or less. If you fall into this category, then you will owe 10% of that income in tax. But if you earn any more than that amount, not every single dollar of the money that you earn may be taxed at the very same percentage.

For instance, single tax filers pay (in 2016) the following tax rates on income:

Single Taxpayer

Taxable Income	Tax Rate
$0 to $9,275	10%
$9,276 to $37,450	$927.50 plus 15% of the amount over $9,275
$37,651 to $91,150	$5,183.75 plus 25% of the amount over $37,650
$91,151 to $190,150	$18,558.75 plus 28% of the amount over $91,150
$190,151 to $413,350	$46,278.75 plus 33% of the amount over $190,150
$413,351 to $415,050	$119,934.75 plus 35% of the amount over $413,350
$415,051 or more	$120,529.75 plus 39.6% of the amount over $415,050

Source: IRS.gov

Using an example, let's say that you actually earn even just $100 more than $9,275, or a total of $9,375. In that case, you would owe 10% tax on the money that falls into the first bracket. So, you would owe 10% on the first $9,275 that you earned (10% X $9,275 = $927.50 in tax).

But then you would also owe 15% on that $100 amount that has spilled over into the next bracket. Income in the next bracket is taxed at 15%. Therefore, the additional $100 that you earned would be taxed at 15%, so you would owe $15 on those earnings. ($100 X 15% = $15 in tax). In total for the year, your taxes would be $942.50. ($927.50 + $15 = $942.50).

Currently, the highest income tax bracket is 39.6%. But, because brackets have changed over the years, it could be that by the time you retire, there may be income tax brackets that are in excess of 40%.

Where your retirement income is generated from will be a key factor. That is because different types of accounts can have different rules on taxation. For instance, money that is generated from tax-deferred accounts such as 401(k)s and Traditional IRAs, will be taxed as ordinary income. And, if you paid into these accounts with pre-tax dollars, then 100% of your withdrawals will be taxed. That is because these dollars have not been previously taxed.

If you do happen to receive retirement income from a defined benefit pension plan, and / or from a government pension, this income is typically all taxable at your ordinary income tax rate (provided that you did not make any after-tax contributions into the plan).

If you take money out of taxable accounts, such as from the sale of stocks, mutual funds, or bonds that are in a personal investment account (i.e., not an IRA or a qualified retirement account), then these funds can be taxed as capital gains.

The length of time that you held these investments will determine whether those capital gains will be considered long-term or short-term. Here, if you have owned the investment for longer than one year, then the money that you withdraw is considered to be long-term for the capital gains tax rate. Many taxpayers pay 15% on long-term capital gains. If, however, in retirement you are in the 10% or the 15% bracket, you could end up paying 0% on these funds.

If you have money in a Roth IRA account, these funds went into the account after-tax. While inside of the account, you received tax-free growth - and, upon withdrawing the money in retirement, you will also pay no tax.

Many people also receive income from annuities in retirement. The tax that you pay on your annuity withdrawals will depend on the portion of your income payment that represents a return of principal and the amount that represents your gain. In this case, the portion that is a return of your principal will be received income tax free. The portion that is considered gain will be taxed at your ordinary income tax rate.

If, however, you have an annuity that has been purchased with pre-tax funds - such as with an annuity that is purchased inside of a Traditional IRA account - then all of your income payment would be considered taxable.

Many people receive Social Security income in retirement, too. Oftentimes, this income is received free of taxation. But, if you earn money in retirement - such as through a part- or a full-time job - and you are also receiving Social Security income benefits, then you may be taxed on a portion of the Social Security benefits that you receive.

For example, in 2016, if your "combined" income is over a certain amount, depending on how you file your tax return, you may be required to pay tax on either 50% or on 85% of your Social Security benefits. (Combined income is determined by taking your adjusted gross income and adding in your non-taxable interest, as well as half of your Social Security income).

If you file your federal tax return as an individual and your combined income is between $25,000 and $34,000, then you may need to pay income tax on up to 50% of your Social Security benefit. If your combined income is more than $34,000, you may need to pay tax on up to 85% of your benefits.

Those who are married and file jointly and who have combined income of between $32,000 and $44,000 will be taxed on up to 50% of their Social Security benefits, and if your income is more than $44,000, then up to 85% of your Social Security benefits may be taxed.[1]

In any case, having to hand over a certain amount of your income in taxes during retirement will obviously have an effect on how much you will actually net out to be used for paying your living expenses. With that in mind, it is essential to plan your retirement income with income taxes in the mix.

Healthcare in Retirement

Even though you may be saving money for the future, the cost of healthcare for those who are retired can be astronomical. In fact, it has been estimated that someone who is age 65 today can expect to spend roughly $130,000 on health and medical related costs throughout their retirement years - and that is even with being insured by Medicare.[2]

This amount includes the many out-of-pocket expenses that a lot of Medicare enrollees are not aware of until they are in the program, which includes a wide array of copayments, coinsurance, and deductibles.

But the $130,000 figure refers to an individuals. So, if you are married, then plan on spending on healthcare for you and your spouse to be in the range of $260,000.[3] How might that affect your lifestyle going forward?

Although many retirees have healthcare coverage through Medicare in retirement, this program can hit you hard with your out-of-pocket responsibility, as well as with items that are not covered.

For example, Original Medicare - which is another name for Medicare Part A and Part B - doesn't provide coverage for some of the items that many retirees need, such as dental and eyeglasses. And, if you want coverage for prescription medication, which is another primary cost for most retirees, you'll have to get that separately, as well, through Medicare Part D.

In order to help pay for some of Medicare's out-of-pocket expenses, you could purchase a Medicare Supplement insurance policy. These policies are specifically geared towards filling in some of the "gaps" in Original Medicare's coverage. (This is why Medicare Supplement is often referred to as Medigap insurance).

There are ten different Medicare Supplement insurance plans - each named after a letter of the alphabet, with Plan A offering the most basic set of "core" benefits. Medicare Supplement insurance is offered through private insurance companies, and not by Medicare itself.

So, while it is required that all Medigap plans of the same letter be structured the same - in other words, the Plan A that you get from one insurer must offer identical benefits to the Plan A that is sold by all other carriers - the premiums can vary substantially from one insurance company to another. With that in mind, it can definitely pay to shop around before purchasing a Medicare Supplement policy.

If you aren't in the best of health, you could also be in luck when it comes to getting Medicare Supplement coverage. That's because, if you apply for a policy during your initial "open enrollment" period, you can't be turned down for coverage, or even charged a higher rate of premium due to your health condition.

Your initial open enrollment period will begin on the first of the month in which you turn age 65, and you are covered by Medicare Part A and B. This period will last for six months. If, however, you wait to apply for Medicare Supplement until after your initial open enrollment period has expired, then you could run the risk of either being charged a higher premium for your pre-existing condition, or not getting the plan you want at all.

Medicare Supplement Insurance Plans (2016)

Medigap Benefits	Medigap Plans									
	A	B	C	D	F*	G	K	L	M	N
Part A coinsurance and hospital costs up to an additional 365 days after Medicare benefits are used up	Yes	Yes	Yes	Yes	Yes	Yes	Yes	Yes	Yes	Yes
Part B coinsurance or copayment	Yes	Yes	Yes	Yes	Yes	Yes	50%	75%	Yes	Yes***
Blood (first 3 pints)	Yes	Yes	Yes	Yes	Yes	Yes	50%	75%	Yes	Yes
Part A hospice care coinsurance or copayment	Yes	Yes	Yes	Yes	Yes	Yes	50%	75%	Yes	Yes
Skilled nursing facility care coinsurance	No	No	Yes	Yes	Yes	Yes	50%	75%	Yes	Yes
Part A deductible	No	Yes	Yes	Yes	Yes	Yes	50%	75%	50%	Yes
Part B deductible	No	No	Yes	No	Yes	No	No	No	No	No
Part B excess charge	No	No	No	No	Yes	Yes	No	No	No	No
Foreign travel exchange (up to plan limits)	No	No	80%	80%	80%	80%	No	No	80%	80%
Out-of-pocket limit**	N/A	N/A	N/A	N/A	N/A	N/A	$4,960	$2,480	N/A	N/A

Plan F also offers a high-deductible plan. If you choose this option, it means that you must pay for Medicare-covered costs up to the deductible amount of $2,180 in 2016 before your Medigap plan pays for anything.

**After you meet your out-of-pocket yearly limit and your yearly Part B deductible, the Medigap plan pays 100% of covered services for the rest of the year.*

***Plan N pays 100% of the Part B coinsurance, except for a copayment of up to $20 for some office visits and up to a $50 copayment for emergency room visits that don't result in inpatient admission.*

For those who live in Massachusetts, Minnesota, or Wisconsin, Medicare Supplement policies are standardized in a different way.

Source: Medicare.gov

As an alternative to being covered by Original Medicare (and a Medicare Supplement insurance plan), you could opt for a Medicare Advantage policy. Medicare Advantage is also referred to as Medicare Part C.

Medicare Advantage policies are also offered via private health insurance companies, so you have the option of shopping around for a plan and a premium that best suits your specific needs.

Medicare Advantage plans must cover the same benefits that are offered in Medicare Parts A and B - but they also offer additional coverage, as well. For example, many Medicare Advantage policies will cover items like vision, dental, and wellness benefits.

Many of these policies will also include prescription drug coverage. Due to the possibility for duplicate coverage, those who are enrolled in Medicare Advantage do not also need Medicare Supplement coverage. In fact, you cannot have both.

There are many different types of Medicare Advantage plans. For instance, some of these plans operate in a similar fashion to HMOs (health maintenance organizations) or PPOs (preferred provider organizations), in that you are limited to a list of healthcare providers in a particular network. You may also need to choose a primary care physician, and obtain a referral prior to seeing a specialist.

Because Medicare Advantage plans are offered through private insurance companies, it is important to compare coverage, as well as the premium cost, before making a decision on a plan. Here, too, you could end up saving money on your outgoing premium expenses, and have fewer surprises in terms of what is and is not covered, by doing so.

In addition to your regular healthcare costs in retirement, there is another component in the health-related area that could have a substantial effect on your income, your assets, and your lifestyle. This component is long-term care.

Although people don't typically like to think about it, the truth is that, as we get older, the chances of needing at least some type of long-term care increase substantially. In fact, according to the U.S. government, a person who is turning age 65 today has almost a 70% chance of needing some type of long-term care services and support in their remaining years.[4]

This care does not come cheaply, either. Based on Genworth's 2016 Cost of Care Survey, in 2016, the average price tag for just one day in a private room in a skilled nursing facility is $253.[5] That adds up to more than $92,000 per year.

Oftentimes, long-term care isn't necessarily required for major illnesses or incapacity. But, it is very common to need assistance with activities like bathing and dressing - even if you receive this care in your very own home. Home health care services are also quite pricy, though - averaging $20 per hour.[6]

On average, a woman will need care for 3.7 years, and a man for 2.2.[7] How many years will your money last if you need long-term care? Having a well-designed plan, which encompasses the potential cost of a long-term care need can help you to ensure that you will be able to obtain the care that you require, while at the same time knowing that your (and your spouse's, if applicable) other living expenses can still be paid.

Sources

1. Social Security Administration
(https://www.ssa.gov/planners/taxes.html)

2. Health Care Costs for Couples in Retirement Rise to an
Estimated $260,000, Fidelity Analysis Shows.
(https://www.fidelity.com/about-fidelity/employer-
services/health-care-costs-for-couples-in-retirement-rise)

3. Ibid.

4. LongTermCare.gov (http://longtermcare.gov/the-basics/how-
much-care-will-you-need/)

5. Genworth Cost of Care Survey 2016.
(https://www.genworth.com/dam/Americas/US/PDFs/Consumer/
corporate/131168_050516.pdf)

6. Ibid.

7. LongTermCare.gov (http://longtermcare.gov/the-basics/how-
much-care-will-you-need/)

Chapter 11: Insurance Needs

In retirement, you not only need to ensure that you have enough income for your expenses, but, it is essential that you protect that income, as well as the assets that you have built up. Otherwise, you could find yourself dipping into your savings - or worse, putting items on credit - if an emergency, a health issue, or other potentially costly event should occur.

In many cases, insurance can help to protect things like your home, your vehicle, and other tangible items, as well as the intangibles, like the high cost of healthcare. You can even insure on ongoing income that will last for a certain number of years, or for the remainder of your entire lifetime, regardless of how long that may be.

Your Health

As we make our way through the journey of life, many people will begin to experience various health issues. While some may be serious, others will just simply require some basic assistance with everyday living activities such as dressing and bathing.

In either case, the cost of future healthcare needs can be astronomical - and, as healthcare expenses continue to rise, it can be devastating to your portfolio unless you have some type of insurance to protect yourself from these high, and continuously increasing, expenses.

Many retirees who are age 65 and over will have Medicare. This program was designed to help pay for healthcare expenses for those who are 65 and older, as well as some individuals who are under age 65 but have a qualifying disability.

Medicare has four components. These include:

- Part A - Hospitalization
- Part B - Doctors' Services
- Part C - Medicare Advantage
- Part D - Prescription Drug Coverage

Medicare Parts A and B are referred to as Original Medicare. This is because, when Medicare was first established back in 1965, these were the only two components. With Original Medicare, you will have coverage for in-patient hospitalization, as well as coverage for doctor visits and other qualifying services. You may also add Medicare Part D, which provides coverage for prescription medication.

Typically, Medicare Part A does not require that you pay a premium. You do need to pay a monthly premium for Medicare Part B, though. For many people, the cost of Medicare Part B (in 2016) is $121.80 per month. However, several years ago, Medicare revised its Part B premium structure. So, if you earn over a certain amount of adjusted gross income (AGI), your premium may be higher.

Medicare Part B Premiums (in 2016)

If your 2014 AGI was this amount, and your file your taxes as an individual:	If your 2014 AGI was this amount, and you file your taxes jointly with a spouse:	If your 2014 AGI was this amount and you are married but file a separate tax return:	You will pay this monthly amount (in 2016) for Medicare Part B premium:
$85,000 or less	$170,000 or less	$85,000 or less	$121.80
Above $85,000 up to $107,000	Above $170,000 up to $214,000	Not applicable	$170.50
Above $107,000 up to $160,000	Above $214,000 up to $320,000	Not applicable	$243.60
Above $160,000 up to $214,000	Above $320,000 up to $428,000	Above $85,000 and up to $129,000	$316.70
Above $214,000	Above $428,000	Above $129,000	$389.80

Source: Medicare.gov

Although Medicare Part A and Part B cover a wide range of services, they also come with a long list of deductibles, copayments, and coinsurance. For many people, these costs can be quite high, depending on how much you need in terms of healthcare services.

Because of that, you can also purchase a Medicare Supplement insurance policy. These plans can help you with filling in Original Medicare's "gaps" in coverage. There are ten Medicare Supplement plans to choose from.

You could alternatively opt for a Medicare Advantage plan. These plans, also known as Medicare Part C, will provide the same benefits that you receive in Original Medicare, as well as additional coverage, such as dental, vision, and wellness. Many Medicare Advantage plans will also include benefits for prescription drug coverage.

If you are not yet age 65 and retired - or if you need additional coverage for healthcare expenses - there are some health insurance options that you may choose from that can help you in bridging the gap before you become eligible for Medicare. These can include COBRA, retiree health insurance, or individual health insurance coverage.

With COBRA (Consolidated Omnibus Reconciliation Act), you may be able to continue the health insurance coverage that you and / or your spouse had via an employer-sponsored group health plan.

Many employers that offer group health insurance benefits to their employees are required to extend those benefits temporarily if the employee has experienced certain changes in their employment status, such as being laid off or terminated, or by voluntarily leaving the company due to early retirement.

Typically, businesses that employ a minimum of 20 employees for at least 50% of the business days in the prior year are required to offer COBRA to those who are no longer considered eligible to participate in the group plan.

If you choose to go this route, you will have the same health insurance benefits that you had while you were covered under the employer's plan. The premium that you will have to pay can vary, but it may not exceed 102% of the standard cost of participating in your employer's group health insurance plan.

Another option for covering your healthcare expense needs may be retiree health insurance that is offered by your former employer. In some cases, employers may provide this type of coverage to retirees.

This retiree health insurance coverage will typically require that the former employee pay an out-of-pocket premium. Unfortunately, many companies have stopped offering these benefits to their retirees due to the high cost of providing the coverage.

You could also consider purchasing your own individual health insurance. While these plans may require a high premium, and they are also oftentimes more difficult to qualify for due to potential risk to the insurer, this can provide you with the temporary protection that you need until you are able to qualify for Medicare.

One way to help with keeping the premium cost of individual health insurance down is to purchase a policy that has a high deductible - and therefore, a lower premium - in conjunction with a Health Savings Account (HSA). You could then use funds from the HSA for qualifying out-of-pocket expenses.

Health Savings Accounts have certain tax advantages in that the money that is contributed into the account can be tax-deductible. These funds may also grow tax-free - and certain types of withdrawals may also be tax-free if they are used for qualified medical expenses.

Long-Term Care

In addition to regular healthcare expenses, there is also a high likelihood that once a person reaches age 65, they will need at least some type of long-term care services. These can be obtained in a facility or at the person's home, depending on their specific needs.

Because the average cost of just one day in a skilled nursing home facility (in 2016) is more than $250[1], the expense of a long-term care need can truly add up. For example, incurring a daily cost of $250 can be more than $90,000 per year. How many years could you continue to pay this cost out-of-pocket? This type of care can be particularly detrimental to couples, when the healthy spouse still needs income to pay his or her regular living expenses. Over a short period of time, many retirees' portfolios can be drained.

In order to cover this type of expense, there are several options. One is to purchase a long-term care insurance policy. These policies can provide coverage for expenses that are incurred in a nursing home facility, as well as for various costs of home health care.

Today, there are also "combination" life insurance / long-term care and annuity / long-term care policies, where the plan will provide life insurance proceeds or annuity income - but, if you need long-term care, you can access the cash within the policy for this, as well.

One of the key criteria in considering long-term care coverage is knowing who you may be able to count on for help if you need it. For instance, in some cases, a parent who requires additional assistance may be able to reside with a family member or other loved one. But, even in these cases, the ultimate cost of a long-term care need can still be devastating to your savings. So, having this protection can be beneficial.

Your Home and Vehicle(s)

When you reach retirement, you will also still need to ensure that assets like your home and your autos are covered. In addition to helping to protect you from the cost of an accident or a disaster such as fire, these policies also provide liability coverage in the case of injury or death to another person. Most states actually require you to purchase auto insurance if you are a licensed driver. The required minimum amount of coverage differs from state to state.

Your Life

Although there are many people who believe that life insurance is no longer needed by retirees, the reality is that there can still be a number of reasons to keep life insurance in force, or even to expand your life insurance coverage in retirement.

Just some of these can include:

- Payoff of Mortgage and / or Other Debts - If you have large debt obligations such as a mortgage, a business loan, and / or credit card balances, then having a life insurance policy in place can provide the proceeds that your loved ones need to pay these off. Otherwise, you could end up leaving debt to those you care about.
- Replacement of Retirement Income for a Spouse - There are many cases where pension or other retirement income sources will either be reduced, or eliminated altogether, when one spouse passes away. This could leave the surviving spouse in immediate financial hardship, with no way to pay their current living expenses. But, the proceeds from a life insurance policy can help to replace the funds that your survivor may need.
- Estate Taxes - Upon passing away, your survivors could be liable for paying estate taxes. A properly constructed plan that includes life insurance can use the policy's proceeds for paying some or all of this estate tax obligation.
- Inheritance - You could need life insurance so as to provide an inheritance to those you love. Policy proceeds may also be used for "evening out" an inheritance. For example, if you have two children, and one of them will inherit a business that you own, but the other has no interest in the business, life insurance proceeds could be left to that child instead.
- Charitable Donation - There are many people who wish to make a charitable donation to an organization that they care about. By providing a charitable entity with the proceeds from a life insurance policy, you can offer the organization a nice amount of tax-free funds for their needs.

- Special Needs - There may also be situations where a retiree has a special needs child or other loved one. If you are caring for someone who may not be able to care for themselves, you will likely want to be sure that their care will extend, even if you are no longer there. Setting up life insurance via a special needs trust can be a great way to provide this. In fact, these plans can often be set up so as not to impede on or disqualify your special needs loved one from any government assistance or other income that they are already receiving.

- Business Succession - If you are the owner or partner in a business, you are probably well aware of just how devastating the loss of a key individual can be to the company. In order to make sure that your business carries on - or is properly sold - life insurance proceeds can be used. For example, the funds from a life insurance policy can be put in place to keep the business afloat until a replacement is obtained. Likewise, policy proceeds may also be used for keeping your business running until a good, qualified buyer is located, or so that the other owners or partners in the business can purchase your share of the company. In addition, if your spouse and / or other family members count on income from your business, life insurance proceeds can be used for providing them with the proceeds to help in replacing such funds.

- Final Expenses - Regardless of one's particular situation, most people will have final expenses when they pass away. These include the cost of a funeral, as well as associated costs, such as a burial plot and head stone. Today, final expenses can be in excess of $10,000 - so, in order to ensure that your loved ones are not saddled with this cost, life insurance proceeds can instead be earmarked for these expenses.

There are many types of life insurance policies available that do not require taking a medical exam in order to qualify. So, even if you have certain health issues, you could still qualify for the coverage that you need.

Your Income

One of the biggest fears on the minds of most retirees today is that of running out of income. There is a long list of potential dangers to retirement income, including market volatility, inflation, healthcare costs, and even longevity.

While there is no way to control the stock market, there is a way to ensure that you will have at least some amount of income receipt for the remainder of your (and also a spouse's, if applicable) lifetime. This is through an annuity.

Annuities are designed to pay out income for a certain period of time, or for the rest of the recipient's life. Because annuities are an insurance product, they can provide guarantees that most other types of financial vehicles cannot.

Because an annuity will also allow two income recipients, using these vehicles for at least a part of your retirement income planning can help you to ensure that both you and your surviving spouse will be able to receive income for as long as it is needed - regardless of how long that may be.

How to Enjoy Life While Spending Less

In retirement, your income and your spending needs will likely change. In some areas, you may spend more after you retire. After all, in retirement, every day can be like Saturday! But, in other cases, it may be that the amount of income that is generated from investments, Social Security, and / or other sources may not be enough to pay for an unlimited amount of expenses. In that case, it may be necessary for you to spend less.

The good news is that, even when spending less, your retirement can be highly enjoyable. According to The Economist, how much we spend throughout our lifetimes can depend in large part on our age. For instance, in many cases, people increase their day-to-day expenditures until reaching middle age. But thereafter, spending will oftentimes drop off.[2]

Based on research from a recent study, it was found that, even though the spending on non-essential items such as travel may increase in retirement, there are three areas where spending typically decreases. These include food, transportation, and "personal care," such as the purchase of new clothing.[3]

And, while spending may decrease for many retirees, there is also a great deal of "opportunity cost" that is experienced in retirement, as well. For instance, because retirees are able to have much more freedom in what they do with their time, it can be well worth it to spend less on items and services in order to have this freedom. In this case, for example, while during your working years, your time may have been affiliated with an hour's worth of pay, retirees are able to enjoy time while not being tied to a clock.[4]

Provided that you have enough income to pay for your essentials, retirement can be an extremely happy time in your life. In order to get to that point, though, it is essential to have a good, solid roadmap in place, and then to follow it to your destination. So, even if you are actually spending less in terms of dollars and cents - if you spend smarter and better, you'll find that your enjoyment in life can increase.

Sources

1. Genworth 2016 Cost of Care Survey

2. Time as money. The Economist. (http://www.economist.com/blogs/freeexchange/2013/08/ageing -and-personal-finance)

3. Ibid.

4. Ibid.

Chapter 12: Figure Out How to Get There

All journeys have both a beginning point and an end point. Starting to save money for retirement is typically the beginning point for most people (unless you are independently wealthy).

It also entails determining when you want to get there, and how well you will live when you do, depending on your available resources. This is where a map and a good solid plan are necessary for ensuring that you get where you want to go, without getting off track.

But retirement – regardless of what age you get there – should not be considered the end of the journey, but rather the beginning. Here, you will have reached the destination that you're been driving towards, possibly for all of your life. So, when you get there, enjoy the rest of the ride! Doing so, however, will also require that you have a good plan in place.

Projecting How Much You Will Need

Truly enjoying the journey of retirement will require you to have enough income to pay your living expenses, as well as to have some fun. While you may have had certain expenses during your working years, the amount of monthly income that you'll need in retirement may not be the same.

This is because there are some expenses that will typically go down, and others that may go up. For instance, while you may not be spending as much in transportation (such as getting to and from work) and in purchasing certain personal items on a regular basis, such as new clothes for work, you will likely see a rise in other areas, such as travel, healthcare, and entertainment.

So, in figuring out the best way to get to your retirement destination, you should first take a look at what your expenses will likely be. Your expenses in retirement will probably include the following:

- Rent or Mortgage (including property taxes, if applicable)
- Utilities
- Healthcare (which includes the cost of your doctor visits, prescriptions, and your health insurance / Medicare premium, as well as your deductible(s) and copayment(s))
- Transportation (fuel, and the cost of a car payment, if you have one)
- Home Maintenance
- Auto Maintenance
- Home Owners Insurance
- Auto Insurance
- Credit Card and / or other Loan Repayment
- Personal Items (such as toiletries, household goods, and clothing)
- Food
- Dining Out
- Entertainment
- Travel
- Life Insurance Premium
- Long-term Care Insurance Premium
- Hobbies
- Gifts
- Charitable Contributions
- Other

Once you have your list of potential living expenses in place, add everything up so that you will get the total amount of incoming cash flow that you will likely require every month. (Be sure to factor in items that you may only pay quarterly, such as your auto insurance. For instance, if you pay $150 each quarter, divide the amount into what you would instead be paying monthly, in order to determine your monthly cost. In this case, it would be $50).

It is also important to keep in mind that some or all of these expenses are likely to go up over time, based on inflation. So, for instance, if you've added everything up and your total monthly outgo comes to $3,000 – but you don't plan to retire for several years – then, you will need to also factor in the potential cost of inflation. Otherwise, you could get to your retirement date and find that you have far more outgoing bills than you had anticipated.

How Much Can You Safely Spend Based on Your Current Resources?

Arriving at your retirement destination will require that you are able to safely spend the amount of money that you need, based on your necessary expenses, as well as for the ancillary items like travel, entertainment, and fun.

Your potential sources of income may include:

- Pension
- Social Security
- 401(k), 403(b) and / or other employer-sponsored retirement plan
- Traditional and / or Roth IRA
- Personal Investments
- Interest / Dividends
- Annuity
- Rental Real Estate
- Reverse Mortgage
- Job (part-time, full-time, or self-employment income)

If you have any income that may only come in sporadically, then be sure to divide the amount into a monthly figure, like you did with your expenses. Also, just as you did with your expenses, once you have your list of retirement income sources, add up the projected amounts in order to determine approximately how much you can count on every month.

When doing so, keep in mind that some or all of your income sources in retirement may still be taxed. For instance, if you continue to work, but you are also receiving income from Social Security, you could have either 50% or 85% of those benefits taxed, depending on how much you earn. Likewise, the income that you earn from a full- or part-time job, as well as from self-employment will be taxed.

In most cases, the income that you receive from your 401(k) and / or Traditional IRA funds will also be taxed. This is because your deposits into these accounts were likely pre-tax. Alternatively, if you receive income from a Roth IRA, this will be tax-free.

Therefore, be sure that you figure potential income and / or capital gains taxes into the equation, and that you come up with your net income. Otherwise, you may find that you won't have enough flowing in.

After you have both your expense and your income figures, subtract the amount of total monthly expenses from the amount of your total projected monthly income. If your result is a positive number, great! That means that you are on the right track and will likely be able to live your desired retirement lifestyle.

If, however, you find that your anticipated income will not be enough to take care of your living expenses in retirement, don't panic. There are some strategies that you can use for either still getting you where you want to go, and / or for taking a detour.

The beauty of having your retirement GPS system is that, even if you happen to run into a road block, you can review alternate routes, and in turn, you can still know exactly how to get where you're going. The earlier you have your plan in place, the more time you will have to determine whether you are on track, and if you need to make any modifications.

Chapter 13: Strategies for Those Who Have Not Saved Enough

When moving closer to retirement, you may find that there is not enough income potential to allow you the lifestyle in retirement that you had hoped for. In this case, while it may require making some adjustments to your route, there are several strategies that you can consider. These can include:

- Continuing to Work / Delay Retirement Date - One strategy that you can use is to simply work longer. This can actually accomplish several things. First, you will be continuing to receive a regular amount of income every month. And, if this amount has been in line with your current living expenses, then you will be able to continue with your present lifestyle.

  Second, this strategy can also allow you to put more towards your Social Security earnings, and in turn, possibly raise the amount of income you will be eligible to receive. Social Security retirement earnings are based in part on your 35 highest-earning years, so this can be particularly beneficial if you are earning more income right now than you have in the past.

- Beginning a New Part- or Full-Time Job - If you want to leave your current line of employment, you could consider starting a new part- or full-time job. This, too, can not only allow you to receive additional income that you'll need, but it can also provide you with the ability to do something different, possibly an endeavor that you have always wanted to try.

- Delaying the Receipt of Social Security Benefits - If you are working, or if you have other income sources that you can count on, you could also opt to delay the receipt of your Social Security benefits. In doing so, each year that you delay between your full retirement age and age 70, you will essentially "earn" an 8% increase in the amount. This increase, known as delayed retirement credits, can make a big difference in your Social Security income benefit amount - especially if you delay taking these benefits for a few years.

- Reducing Your Monthly (or Your Permanent Ongoing) Expenses - Certainly, another option would be to reduce your expenses. This could mean doing away with certain travel plans or other potential goals such as purchasing a vacation home. In many cases, though, you can find areas in your monthly budget to decrease, without having to make too much of a lifestyle change going forward. For example, if you are married and both you and your spouse own a car, then you could cut back to having just one vehicle. This could cut out the cost of the vehicle itself, as well as other ancillary expenses such as auto insurance coverage.

Portfolio Allocation

Because everyone's retirement goals are not exactly the same, it is important that the financial products inside of your portfolio are properly allocated, based on what you need them to do, and where exactly you are on your journey. While all financial assets may be good for certain purposes, they may not all be right for you and your specific goals. That is why it is essential to place assets into the proper asset allocation categories.

There are several different levels of asset allocation, and this will typically differ based upon the safety and the volatility of the various asset categories. This is why asset allocation is often referred to as a pyramid, with the "safer" assets making up a strong and stable foundation, and the more aggressive growth-oriented assets that may entail more risk being situated at the top.

Asset Allocation Pyramid

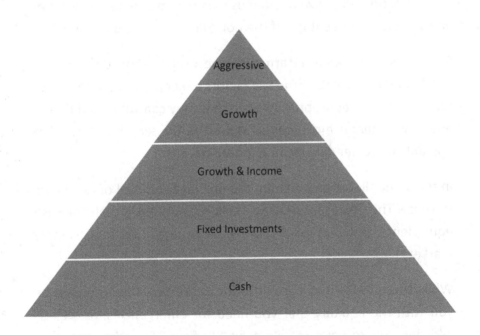

As an example, investors who are younger and may have a long time before they reach retirement, will often have a larger percentage of their portfolio invested in growth and / or aggressive growth vehicles. These types of assets can provide the opportunity for nice gains. However, they also can be more risky. So, if their value does decrease, younger investors will generally have more time to recoup from these down times.

When approaching retirement, safety of principal can become more of an issue. With that in mind, it is typically wise to move a larger percentage of your assets into the "safer" categories such as growth & income, and even fixed investments.

As you enter into retirement, and you will require income from your investments to live on, in most cases, it makes sense to move an even larger percentage of the portfolio into fixed investments.

So, in essence, when determining the proper allocation of your portfolio's assets, one of the key factors to keep in mind is that your funds should be appropriated such that they can withstand the up and down market movements, as well as the length of time that you anticipate needing income in retirement.

In the asset allocation pyramid, the first layer or level of assets are the base. This represents having a solid foundation of cash and cash equivalents, such as bank savings accounts, CDs, and money markets.

While these funds may earn little (or no) return, they can provide you with the liquidity that you need for emergencies, as well as allowing you to have readily available funds for other potential investment opportunities.

Even though the base of the pyramid can provide you with safety of principal, though, it is important to be careful not to allocate too high of a percentage of assets in this particular category. That's because the return that you are generating in this area will not usually keep up with ongoing inflation.

The second level of the asset allocation pyramid is fixed investments. The investment vehicles that are placed into this area can provide you with income, as well as safety of principal, as they do not carry a high amount of risk. Some of the options that are included in this level are government bonds and Treasuries.

The third level is growth and income. This may add a bit more volatility to the overall portfolio. However, it can be in exchange for offering both current income, as well as the opportunity for your principal to grow - often somewhat more than the rate of inflation.

Moving higher up the pyramid, the fourth level is growth. Growth vehicles are those that can offer the opportunity for yet a higher return, albeit a bit more volatility. Investments in this category can typically include individual growth stocks, growth stock mutual funds, variable annuities, and stock unit trusts.

Because of their potential for a higher return, it is important that, even in retirement, you have at least some percentage of your portfolio here, as these vehicles can provide the growth that is needed to outpace inflation, as well as for keeping the portfolio intact over a longer period of time once you begin to draw down income from it.

At the top of the pyramid you will find aggressive growth assets. These are the type of alternatives that can offer a great deal of return, however, in exchange for that, there can also be more risk to your principal. Here you may find small cap stocks, aggressive unit trusts, and emerging market mutual funds.

Over time, the assets that are in your portfolio will typically need to be reviewed and re-allocated. By regularly taking a close look at your overall portfolio, and on how it is performing based on your needs, you will be able to determine whether or not you are moving in the right direction. And, if you do look to be off course, moving assets into different categories can often provide the solution that you need.

For example, because life is always in a state of change, it is important that you regularly look behind, ahead, and both ways as you travel towards retirement and you are making your financial decisions. Ideally, you should review your allocation of assets at least once per year - or more often, if you have encountered a major life change.

Such changes can include experiences such as marriage or divorce, the birth of a child or a grandchild, a death in the family, the loss of employment, and / or the purchase or sale of a business. Any of these situations can impact both your current and your future financial scenario.

How Much Risk Tolerance Do You Have?

In addition to allocating assets based on the time period of your life, as well as on your financial goals, another key component of where your specific assets should be placed in the asset allocation pyramid will be dependent on your risk tolerance.

Along with your overall goals and the stage that you are in your life, the tolerance that you have for risk in your investments will also play a key role in how and where you should ideally place your funds.

For some people, the ups and downs of the roller coaster stock market may keep them awake at night, while for others, the potential opportunity for growth may be well worth the ride - even if it takes some volatility in order to get there.

Prior to going into any type of financial vehicle, it will be essential, then, that you are willing and able to stomach large swings in your returns and / or you are ok with safer options, knowing that your principal will remain in-tact.

One of the best ways to remain active across a broad spectrum of assets, while at the same time helping you to reduce risk, is by diversifying your investments. Investopedia defines diversification as being "a risk management technique that mixes a wide variety of investments within a portfolio."

The rationale behind diversification contends that a portfolio that has different types of investments will, on average, yield higher returns as well as pose a lower amount of risk than any of the individual investments that are within the portfolio.

So, spreading your investments across a wide range of options can be a good way for you to reduce your risk along your journey, while also allowing you to drive faster than just the minimum speed limit.

Planning for Expensive Scenarios

When traveling on a long trip, you will typically find that there will be some bumps along the road. For instance, you may get a flat tire and need to replace it with the spare. Or, you may find that your entire transmission in out of whack and it requires you to put your car in the shop for a while - typically with a large payment due in order to continue on your way.

In the case of planning for retirement, these bumps could include the need for extended healthcare or an unexpected rise in the price of items that you regularly purchase and use. In this case, planning ahead is essential.

Some situations will allow for insurance coverage to help with paying some or all of the cost. In other scenarios, though, it may entail that you have an ample emergency fund set aside for "just in case." It may also require that you have set up your retirement income so as to increase over time. Doing so can help you to ensure that your income will still be in line with your rising expenses in the future.

Having to alter or rearrange your retirement planning doesn't always mean that the situation is negative, though. For instance, you might have a dream of purchasing a home on the beach, or buying a nice RV so that you can travel the country on your own terms.

For these types of situations, it will require that you set clear goals up front so that you know what it will entail to get where you want to go - not just to "retirement" in general, but to the unique goals and dreams that you have set for your future life.

Retirement is a time to have fun and enjoy life. While it will require that you have an ongoing - and rising - income in order to pay your expenses, and it may also come with some unexpected monetary needs, if you have set your sights on where you are going and on what it will take to get there, then you are likely to remain on track throughout your trip.

Conclusion

As with any type of long journey, the planning of your retirement needs to be approached with a starting point, a destination, and a map that can get you from here to there. Setting clear cut goals, as well as knowing what your purpose in retirement will be, are key indicators that can help to point you in the right direction along the way.

Likewise, by regularly reviewing your map and its coordinates, you will be much better able to ensure that you are headed in the right direction - and, if you are off track or run into a detour, it won't knock you completely off track and too far off of your course.

By using the GPS system, you will be able to look clearly at your overall retirement planning picture, as well as each individual leg of your journey. Sometimes, a long journey with a big goal at the end can seem a bit overwhelming. But, the GPS system can help you to break down your route into smaller segments that can be much more easily focused on.

This can be particularly helpful if you should happen to run into unexpected "bad weather" along the route, such as market volatility, low interest rates, and / or a costly healthcare or emergency expense.

The road conditions may not always be ideal, and you may find that there is construction along the way, but knowing that you are on the right path can make all the difference in the world - not only when you arrive at where you're going, but throughout the entire ride.

Just as the old saying goes, every journey begins with a single step. So, whether you are in the early process of planning for your retirement, or if the road that you are currently on doesn't seem to be taking you to the right place, then the GPS Method may be what you need in order to ensure that you get back on the right road and ultimately arrive safely at your desired goal.

Regardless of where you are on the road to retirement right now, I hope that you find success. The road can be long, but the scenery and the stops along the way can be priceless. If you would like more information on the GPS Method and/or on how you can program in the right route to your retirement destination, ken@mahoneygps.com for additional information.